Reckoning 7

Reckoning 7
Electronic Edition: Winter 2023
Print Edition: Summer 2023

Cover and interior ornament by Elsie Andrewes

Reckoning Press
206 East Flint Street
Lake Orion, MI 48362
www.reckoning.press
distributed by IngramSpark

 ISSN 2474-7327
e-ISBN 978-1-955360-08-1
ISBN 978-1-955360-09-8

Contents

Cover:
Drua

Elsie Andrewes

Elsie Andrewes. Fiji born artist and illustrator based in Whangārei, Aotearoa/New Zealand. Works span across traditional and digital media, covering portraiture, botanical illustrations and surrealist concepts with inspiration stemming from my heritage.

Most pieces are completed with the Pacific people in mind and for the Pacific people, utilising vibrant colours and traditional design. I've been commissioned by the World Bank, Talanoa, Huia Publishers, and Witness Performance. Have also exhibited at Enjoy Contemporary Gallery in Wellington. You'll find me in a cafe somewhere drinking a flat white or at beach. Vinaka

Photo credit: Vivien Beduya

From the Editors

Priya Chand

Water: what is it good for? Absolutely everything.

(I'm sorry. But also not. I hope that's stuck in your head now.)

In privileged areas worldwide, access to clean water is never far away. Water is so ubiquitous—and, depending where you live, so seemingly renewable—that, if you are in this population, it's easy to forget how easily disrupted these systems are, how quickly that convenient tap can go from potable to unsafe, how your recreational or work sites can be shut down or disrupted practically overnight.

I'm excited for all of you to read four perspectives that are as diverse as the challenges facing our water systems today. Each piece brings an environmental issue into stark personal focus. Whether it's government or paramilitary action, the exploitation of resources far past what can be sustained, or the ever-lurking shadow of global warming, ecosystems are being transformed at unprecedented rates—and the people who inhabit these ecosystems alongside them.

But these are not stories of hopelessness. Part of focusing on the personal—my favorite part—is that it highlights points where individual action does make a difference. It's easy to look at the challenges today and walk away thinking there is nothing to be done, but that elides the important work that people are doing every single day to protect and restore their communities.

Building resilience matters. If we want to restore natural continuity, we must start by ensuring our spaces—the full ecosystems, including the human elements—are healthy.

Priya Chand is a California transplant living in the Midwest, where she volunteers as a forest steward. Her work is inspired by a background in biology, and has appeared in magazines including *The Magazine of Fantasy & Science Fiction* and *Clarkesworld*.

From the Editors

Tim Fab-Eme

We are so used to statistics that many of us rarely bother about the numbers and what they really mean until alarms trigger us to act. We rarely drink the right amounts of water even when we dread heat injuries, cerebral edema, urinary and kidney problems, seizures, and hypovolemic shocks. The poems in this issue are like a sensor for diagnosing water levels and the impact not only on our personal body but also on our real body—the Earth.

Human activities are increasingly unsettling water bodies everywhere—the Colorado River recedes revealing remains of the Vegas mob families—the Danube empties unveiling carcasses of World War II German warships—the Tiber falls low, showing the stone supports for Nero's Bridge—the Po dries up leaving behind World War II tanks—the Elbe ebbs exhibiting an ancient hunger stone with the inscription: "if you see me, then weep." And we have seen it and we cannot hide the tears falling as broken pieces of the graveyards, dinosaur footprints, settlements, gardens, and the other artifacts vomited by the waters turning toward other places. Because the amount of water in, on, and above the Earth is constant, changes in climate also mean that other rivers are experiencing more rainfall and flood, like the Amazon, the Nile, the Mississippi, the Yangtze, and the Murray.

These poems portray the precarious state of our waterways—from chemical to oil spills, from radioactive to nuclear waste, from invasive to endangered species—and it is not getting any better. Yet we cannot despair. Let us listen to these songs and reconsider our connectedness with the oceans, aquifers and springs, rivers and streams, wetlands, bays, and estuaries that are a part of us. Our body is fragile, our planet is fragile, and both of them are about two-thirds water. These poets, like physicians, have diagnosed our ailments and are calling us to reconsider our activities and care for our body, earth.

Tim Fab-Eme is an engineer and poet who experiments with poetic forms on environmental and social justice themes. He's the Issue 7 poetry editor of *Reckoning: Creative Writing on Environmental Justice*, and Cove Park's 2022 funded writer-in-residence on climate action. Tim loves exploring nature, gardening, and fishing in the mangrove swamps of his island home, Egun-Okom (Ogonokom). His work has appeared in *The Malahat Review*, *The Fiddlehead*, *Magma*, *New Welsh Reader*, *About Place Journal*, *Reckoning: Creative Writing on Environmental Justice*, *Channel: Ireland's Environmental Literary Journal*; *apt*, *Planet in Crisis Anthology*, *Deep Wild Journal: Writing from the Backcountry*, *Land and Territory Anthology*, *Delmarva Review*, *FIYAH*, *The Future of Black: An Afrofuturism & Black Comics Poetry Anthology*, *Borderlands: Texas Poetry Review*, *FU Review*, *The Maine Review*, etc. His other projects center on the lore, myth, and experiences of marginalized folks and communities.

From the Editors

Octavia Cade

I grew up on the coast. That's not unusual, coming from an island country as I do. Water is part of the daily life of islands, beyond the ways of drinking and planting that are common to all of us. Nearly every week my parents would take my sister and me down to the beach to play in the rock pools. The intertidal zone is something I never grew out of, and the sense memory of salt water and salted rock, the way they felt on my fingertips, is something I can easily call up.

There is something particularly relevant about those rock pools. They're so easy to influence. All the little crabs and starfish, all the sea lettuce and Neptune's necklace. My sister and I could have scoured it all out if we wanted to. We could have smashed the sharp-slicing baby mussels that lined the rocks. The pools could be so small that even as children we were large enough to outmatch them. What we didn't realise, as children, was how tolerant rock pools are. The organisms that live there are adapted to such extremes. Their environment changes in salinity, in temperature, in exposure to sunlight, and in turbulence. There's so much that they can survive . . . and then there was us, with our buckets and our ice-creams, ready to explore. Ready to *shape*.

That's what the stories of this issue do. I think of them as rock pools, as little worlds with their authors standing over them, sunburned and observant. Maybe they don't have ice-cream or those bright little buckets with them, but they're still watching, because rock pools are places of wonder and of living with change. If we watch them closely enough, through that clear bright lens of water, we can learn to be adaptive too.

Octavia Cade is a New Zealand speculative fiction writer. She has a PhD in science communication, and a particular interest in climate fiction. She's the 2023 Ursula Bethell writer in residence at the University of Canterbury, where she'll be writing a series of creative nonfiction essays about NZ ecology. Her latest book, *The Impossible Resurrection of Grief*, was published in 2021 by Stelliform Press.

The Bright in the Gyre

Nadine Aurora Tabing

Near the end of the last year of her projected life expectancy, Cora knows she shouldn't be spending any moment on frivolities. Her store of oxygen tanks is depleting. Her body begins wheezing halfway up the stairs to her apartment. Every last breath in her body needs to be spent on work, on microscopes and slideshows and documentation and the full spectrum of mycelium she's endeavored so hard to engineer.

But instead of thinking about any of this, she, like everyone else, is riveted to her newsfeed. She clings to every eddy of information.

The satellites spot them first at night: lights where there should be none, sparse enough to be mistaken for dead pixels in the ocean's inky gut. Before long, the lights splatter into a constellation orbiting 32°N and 145°W, and those who know the significance of that migratory path are summoned to interviews that flood every social media feed.

WHAT IS IN THE NORTH PACIFIC GYRE?

There's speculation, amazement, alarm. Journalists and researchers and influencers livestream their journeys by sea and sky toward the light, cameras panning across the ocean's seemingly endless blue, and then its seemingly endless heaving crust of bags, bottles, rope. Even that far out from the coast, the currents gleam in rainbow neons from runoff. Telephoto lenses show a reusable straw jabbing skyward like an arm waving for rescue. Snap-lid plastic tubs bob like polygonal turtle shells, one of which is lifted and upturned by a reporter with a waterplane, revealing barnacles fisted underneath, alive, floating: foreshadowing.

"There are *people* living out here," says the only influencer Cora follows, a girl who speaks in awe through a branded lavender nasal cannula. Self-consciously, Cora adjusts her own, and takes a steadying breath as she zooms her phone camera in on grainy, irregular silhouettes in the ocean's distance.

Over the next weeks, the extent of the floater colony becomes clear. Boats of all models slung to rafts slung to bridges slung to shelters of all sizes, constructed of plastic bottles stuffed with salt-crusted litter and compressed into bricks. A panoply of desalination vats and solar panels bob alongside, dappled with flags, indicating the floaters' various origins. They range from disillusioned tech heirs to typhooned refugees floated out to sea alongside the ruins of sub-sea-level cities. At night, the Gyre rekindles the ocean's horizon, radiating gold and crimson from headlights and lanterns and bulbs on hefty rubber wire.

It's—inspiring.

The monitor in the lab breakroom remains fixed on Gyre newstreams, for hatewatching.

Cora's project manager: "Do they really think they can stay out there forever?"

One of the marketing people: "Living the material-free, zero-waste lifestyle on a luxury yacht—"

An intern, laughing, eager to fit in: "All that garbage they say they hate so much—where do they think all of it is coming from, now?"

Cora feels the words whirl in her belly, coalescing into a hard, sharp knot. It swells. It hurts.

I don't know, she wants to say. *When a storm washed me out to sea as a child, I think I would have been alright ending up there.*

She shuts her eyes.

Focus. Her air is too precious to waste on arguments. She adjusts her cannula, tries to calm down, stares at the news. Overhead, an influencer grimaces and laughs as she rates the output of the Gyre's pelagic forage: slurry stewed with amphipods netted and flash-sanitized from beneath the ocean's crusty skin, snails chopped raw with microgreens raised in a greenhousing boat, fish dried on solar-heated racks.

"Cora," someone calls. It's her boss. "Let's do our dry run."

A withdrawal. In the hallway, Cora's boss starts talking in Tagalog.

"You've been spending a lot of time on Gyre news," he says, "Cora, you need to focus on here and now," and this time, she can't help her protest.

"But—solar panels—mariculture—*housing*—"

There's even more she wants to say: *Anyone that makes it out there gets space, and everyone there is sifting the ocean clean, and it's not just the rich, there are people like me, or people who just didn't want to pay rent, and scientists, everyone who left the field because they couldn't find investors but finally have the dedicated community, and* actual *applications—*

But she can't continue. Those first words were her limit, the only sounds that her deepest breath can inflate. She gags and coughs, and her boss lays a sympathetic hand on her shoulder.

"They've—done more good—than we have—in *years*," Cora forces herself to spit out, and he frowns.

"Our work comes to fruition *today*, Cora. You're willing to throw it all away because of a handful of—sea hippies? Cora," he says finally, "*focus*," and it's these final words that sink into her like lead, sealing her mouth tight behind them.

Focus.

So close to the end, she can't risk being pulled off this project. The path has been so hard—convincing her boss to have a spot on his team—begging allowance to work from home during flareups—nodding her head in every meeting, holding her head up over office gossip about the tank she rolls with her on bad days. She has no illusions; even with her GPA and degrees and circlet of prestigious scholarships, she's the kind of person a lab of this caliber and venture backing took only to improve their diversity numbers. It was challenging work—and, Luis scoffed, relentless—but her best chance at getting what she really wanted.

I want to do something with my life, she wrote on her cover letter. *I want to be the last to suffer this way. I want to die in peace.*

She got the job.

They review the presentation one last time; and then, later that afternoon, in front of the board of directors, Cora's boss recites points from their slideshow flawlessly. Mycolution's arsenal of fungi is ready for deployment. Exhaustive experiments and projections show their full set of offerings is capable of digesting over eighty percent of humanity's most non-degradable waste products, reducing even the most ancient plastics to harmless, reasonably edible mushrooms. Observers can even see the mycelium working: engineered luminescence indicates where hyphae have detected, and are digesting, plastic-based nutrients. Cora displays the diorama on the conference table, three acrylic boxes filled with her best specimen, tweaked and optimized. Each box contains different debris collected from the beach, left with the mycelium for half a year. Someone turns off the lights, for better visibility. Threading through the waste in each box is a lacework of vivid, fervent violet.

This is by far the most impressive demonstration their lab has ever been able to yield—but no one is interested. Cora's chest tightens as one of the board interrupts the presentation halfway through and spends the remainder of the time on interrogation. The developed fungi varieties are fine, but how would the mycelium be transported to landfills? How could companies select the proper species to digest each dump's specific stew of pesticides and nurdles and retired polyester clothing? What appeal was there for a company to wait decades before they could advertise having made any meaningful dent on the planet's health? The costs in time and money and effort were high—there weren't any subsidies for technology this new—and what would be the psychological cost, of bringing back to public consciousness the existence of a bunch of evacuated wastelands that public relations companies had already successfully hidden from view?

Cora gapes. Are they... *serious?* Just because problems are hidden or take a long time to resolve don't mean they aren't *affecting anyone*. It's exactly because of companies making decisions like this that she has had to spend her life like this, not just in pain, but just trying to—*clean up*—

Focus, she tells herself, *focus, be calm, focus*, but her head is heating, and her chest is tightening, and all at once she dissolves, into coughing so harsh that she loses her balance—pitches into a wall—gasps, her breathing awful, *inoutinoutinoutinoutinout.*

In the end, her boss looks relieved at her struggling. It's the perfect excuse to end the meeting.

The next day, she can't even get up from bed. Her head spins. She fumbles herself together just enough message her boss that she's too sick to come in, and accepts his immediate return voice call.

"I know you're discouraged," he says. "But the mycelium aren't completely shelved. Let's do the marketing research, find the money, and try again."

I've already done the research, Cora types back. Her eyes are sore with it, with not sleeping, not resting. *Everything they mentioned, the zero-waste certifications, the focus group branding. It takes a lot of time. More than I have left.*

"None of us will *ever* see the fruit of our labor," her boss argues. "*All* of this work is always for a future we'll never see." But he knows what she really means, and adds: "I don't want to hear you sound so hopeless. This place has good coverage. You'll live as long as anyone else. Just rest, and come back when you're feeling better, alright?"

The way he says it, he's forgotten that this is the only day of paid-time-off she reserves for herself shamelessly every year. She was supposed to spend her birthday in celebration of the project taking off; and in relaxation, one final breather before she dedicated herself to assembling all her documentation for whoever would inherit her work. She isn't supposed to be shuddering nauseous on her couch—dizzy with reviewing PDFs about market and government certifications—nearly collapsing after opening the door for Luis, who arrives with birthday cake. She tries to hold herself together when the candles light, but her tears spatter on the icing. Her body squeaks, struggling to refill after she fails to blow out every candle.

I think, Cora wants to say, *that this is it*—but she can't say it, her body judders, *inoutinoutinoutinout,* and Luis hugs her, holds her face to their chest. They understand.

In the end, Luis's mother also hadn't been able to blow out her candles. It all happened fast, after that.

"All I—want—is one more—year," Cora sobs between breaths. "Just to—to know—that I—"

Luis's arms around her tighten.

"Cora," they say. "You've done all that you could. Please—*please*—just let go of the work. If this is really . . . you know I'll be with you, until the end. But if this is really it . . . I can't bear to see you spend your last days like this. You've done enough."

No. She hadn't managed even *close* to enough. But any protest Cora might have then is interrupted by her buzzing phone. A news alert, for the Gyre: another interview, about water purification methods they're experimenting with. And their new coordinates, near mainland. The alert displays above her boss's last message, a reiteration: *Come back tomorrow when you're feeling better.*

Luis sees the message. "*Don't*," they say. Their voice is low with contempt. "Let's just enjoy the time we have left. They don't deserve your labor, much less you."

They don't, Cora agrees with a shake of her head. Still, she keeps looking at her phone. Her hand, shaking on her oxygen tubing, fists.

"Luis," she says. "You—mean it? With me—until—the end?"

Luis meets her gaze, trying to understand the turn of her voice. Slowly, they nod.

"Okay," Cora says. "Then—I think—I'll go back."

Just one last time.

She met Luis in the university hospital as a teen, back when no one knew the name of what was killing her. She was an orphan, a refugee of Tropical Storm Bagwis, jobless, a student. For her, and for Luis's mother, the stipend given in exchange for their cooperation was better than nothing, and adhering to experiment protocols was well worth the hope they might one day breathe freely, rather than only in spurts, at times sucking for air like fish out of water.

Doctors barraged them with tests, and chased the symptoms around and down to their roots: the blood vessels that branched and withered over and over again in their lungs, like the boughs of trees in manic seasons. That wild growth and anti-growth was thanks to a frantic pendulum of hormones; and *that* was thanks to the chemicals leeched into their bloodstreams by plastics, apparently ingested in fatal levels by both Cora and Luis's mother. They were too numerous and minuscule to extract or neutralize. Luis, who always hated seafood even when it was fried anonymously into bacalaitos, remained unaffected, though it wasn't obvious from how they cried and hugged their mother and Cora both upon official diagnosis.

The news coined their own name for it, vulgar and catchy: *trash lung*. An islander's affliction, carried by superstorm exiles along with whatever baggies of memory cards and soggy photo prints they could keep hold of, adrift, before being scooped up by rescue boats. It felt unfair that the city was where things were safe to eat, with its meat trucked in from toxic mass production facilities. It felt criminal that Cora's poison was bangús she chose from the market alongside her mother, fried and eaten with rice, plain and simple and miasmatic with microplastics and pollution finer than fish bones, and sticking deeper in the throat.

The injustice was obvious. Luis's mother died; and Cora picked them up from their grief, cooked food, helped parse out all the bills, now in Luis's name. It was like the sickness had simply *happened*, with no one to blame: no paper trails, no culprits, and no cures. When Cora asked, the doctors told her that the funding had dried up.

"And what about us?" Cora demanded. "All us research subjects? And what about everyone else in the world that has this?"

I know you're discouraged, was all they said. *Let's just find the money, and try again.*

They told her that she had a while yet—at least until age twenty-eight. She waited, and then she didn't. She wasn't going to die having done nothing. She'd heard of a lab, run by someone from her same hometown, who was trying to use the earth to purify the water.

Presently, Luis searches the chat forums while she makes her final preparations.

And I found someone, they message. *On a Gyre forum. Their boat can take us out to the coordinates the Gyre announced they'd be at in a week. I got the time off. Do you think you have that amount of time?*

Yes, Cora responds.

There's a pause. Luis says, *And you're sure you want to do this?*

Yes, Cora repeats.

And to her own body she begs: *Seven more days. That's it. All I want is seven more days.*

All her life, she's had to balance so much: insurance, co-pays, tuition, grants, rent, oxygen. So it's a blessing, really, that none of that matters at all, anymore. Her life has only one last to-do item.

She heads back to work—after hours, after packing her things, and after connecting herself to a fresh tank. Despite her conviction, her hands shake. The substrate drawers rattle as she opens them—in her anxiety, she accidentally opens one against her tank roller, causing it to clank against a cabinet—and when she finally rights it, and starts to palm a bit of spore-laden substrate into a spare vial, the vial slips, and when she tries to catch it her wild hand instead smashes it.

The sound pierces, echoes. Her breathing goes into overdrive, and then stops: *Inout—in.* In the silence, even the sound of her blood dripping from her palm sounds like a drum. But no one comes when she tamps the soil and spores into the vials with her bleeding hand. No one comes when she slips the vials into her pockets, sock-padded to quiet the clinking. No one comes when she heads out the door. Luis picks her up at the lab's back door, and inside the car is Peregrin, a tanned white woman with a catamaran and a wealth of optimism, who on short notice agreed to delay her departure just another day. They make introductions. At the moorage, Peregrin points at the water, which is scaly with wrappers and plastic bottles and gleams magenta in the moonlight.

"So you've got *mushrooms* that can eat this stuff?"

"Wait," Luis says. Cora is wheezing already, with the effort of walking across the pier. In the catamaran, Peregrin helps her into a seat, and by the time they've made it out of the sound, Cora's pained but steady breathing is deafened by the groan of the boat, the hiss of seafoam on the windows.

Inside her single bag is two changes of clothing, her laptop, and binder-sized substrate trays, with humidifier layers and battery-powered warming elements. Each tray is speckled with various kinds of plastic waste, and labeled according to which mycelium can digest it. It's equipment from home, things she used in the past to continue research over the weekend. She takes a deep breath.

"Yes—they can—eat it," Cora answers finally. "Let me—show you."

The soil in the vials is studded with spores and fluffy hyphae that, once the lights are off, glow: purple, tangerine, cyan, neon jade. On some vials spores luminesce in whorl-shapes, stamped by Cora's thumb. On others, there are smears of blood.

"*Cora,*" Luis gasps. "When did you cut yourself?"

"It's nothing." Her palm is still bleeding, even stinging, sharply—but a brief glance shows her no shards of vial glass, just a little dirt.

"It's not nothing! Cora—"

Cora frowns at them. *This is the least of my worries.* But she accepts antibiotics and a bandage that Peregrin procures from a cabinet, and then returns to work, upending the vials and stirs the spores into the trays. Peregrin peers over Cora's shoulders, impressed.

"That's it? That dirt?"

Cora nods.

"That is *so* fucking cool, Cora," Peregrin laughs. "This stuff *definitely* deserves to be out in the Gyre, rather than in corporate purgatory. You're a goddamn hero. Honestly, I'm honored y'all chose me to help you. Count me in until the end."

Thanks for helping, Cora writes. And then, not wanting to get distracted: *As long these mycelium have nutrients, they're fine anywhere. A toxic dump. An ocean.*

That night, she focuses, and writes everything she can remember about mycelium, about hyphae, about enzymes, polymers, monomers. About detergents and fuel and polystyrene. About how the eventual luminescent caps can be eaten, with no adverse affect whatsoever. It's useful—it *deserves* a life out there. She stays up the whole night, drawing diagrams, arranging files.

All I want, she thinks the next morning, *is six more days.*

"How about taking a break?" Luis asks, halfway through the next day, when she asks them to roll down another tank from her meager storage. "Just for an afternoon? Just for an hour? Just for the sunset?"

No, Cora writes. *I have to focus.*

So close to the end, she can't risk this falling through the cracks, can't risk the last moment of her life being filled with regret. Peregrin brings cut apples as Cora is writing about optimal temperature ranges. Luis brings another air tank as Cora is writing about instructions for how to mix new substrate. Cora writes and writes, and when she starts slowing down on facts, she starts adding dreams, describing training the mycelium's fibrous body into brick-shaped molds, describing a glowing city fruiting on the ocean, stretching, chewing the Great Pacific Garbage Patch up and spitting it out as homes, or at least as floating mycelium reefs.

To actually construct something out of material like that would take years, if not decades, of course—and who knows how it would all fare long-term, in the harsh salt and sun of the Gyre—but she can see it all so clearly, which is a blessing, because if any of this ever became reality, it would be long after her death.

Which is fine, she thinks firmly, *it's fine, it's fine, it's fine*, and she steels herself as she feels her body constrict again—*inoutinoutinout.*

At the end of Luis's mother's life, these attacks had come on so fast and close together that she'd deflated in the space of a week. Gasping, eyes watering, Cora pinches her cut thumb, comforted by the simple sharp pain of it.

All I want is five more days.

By the time the boat noses through water cloudy with polyethylene bags, Cora feels a stab of relief—*We must be close!* But this delight breaks as the day proceeds and the seamless blue of their journey turns murky, then blistered, with debris. A two-second dip of Peregrin's landing net yields handfuls of waste: salt-blunted chips of white and gray and blue plastic, flakes of wave-softened styrofoam. She upends it all onto the deck, and three of them pick through it, with gloves, and morbid curiosity. For a moment Cora raises her hand and wills her fingers to drift and rest, prophetic, on something scattered by a lola or even older ancestor: maybe a family photograph storm-flung by some miracle, through decades and miles, to her possession, an omen, a sign that someone approves of how she's chosen to live and die. But most of the stuff is slimy knots of trawling net, and tatters of fluorescent fishing rope: castoff sloughed off secretly, before it could be counted by an expense report.

Luis is somberly silent. Peregrin wipes her eyes.

"It's different," she murmurs. "When you see it in person."

Cora nods, not wanting to waste air on a useless, depressed *Yes*. The sight of all this garbage, scabbed over the ocean and never healing, congeals in her like she sometimes imagines the plastic inside her does: not ruining her through some haywire of hormones but with something even more basic, as if the blame for her weakening body rests on crackling film and crumbling egg crates lodged between every capillary, too deep for fingers or fine instruments to wedge out. Thinking about it, she feels her chest tighten again, with a kind of claustrophobia—she scratches her skin, as if she could claw the poison inside her out—her cut palm catches on something, and bleeds anew, and the color is so wildly bright and spills so fast and for a moment she feels her chest going again, *inoutinoutinoutin*—

When she returns to consciousness, it's in panic.

Luis, she tries to scream, and she feels her hand, gripped. Luis is in chair beside her hammock; Peregrin is standing over, as well. Both are teary.

"Hey, girl," Peregrin says. "How are you?"

Fine, Cora mouths. She reaches her arm out, toward her laptop, but Luis takes her hand, and squeezes it.

"Cora," they say, "I think you've done enough," and for the first time, Cora can't find the energy to argue. She slumps.

"There are nurses in the Gyre," Peregrin whispers. "Doctors too, maybe. You think maybe one of them could help her? I don't know, I mean—if they could even buy her just another month, or—"

"Maybe," Luis says, and then turns back to Cora, making a smile. "Just four more days. Hang in there, Cora. This—this isn't how you're supposed to go. Don't you . . . do you want to see the Gyre? Isn't that worth staying here for, just a glimpse of it? You have to see it. You have to see where your work will go. Don't you?"

Their eyes are red.

I'll try, Cora mouths, because she knows they'd only protest if she said, *I'm sorry you have to watch this happen all over again. You don't deserve this.*

Luis brushes her hair. "You've done enough," they say, "just rest now, just sleep," and for the first time, it's the easiest thing in the world to do.

Maybe Luis is right.

I've done everything I needed.

I've done everything I could.

I can die now, in peace—

But in the days and hours before her death, robbed of the lush distraction of work, all she can think about is how hard it is to breathe. How cold she feels, even with Peregrin's hand-knit shawl. How her whole body aches, especially her cut hand, even her whole arm. How Luis's mother, in her deathbed, had painkillers, and movies, and short books—but all Cora has is an ache deeper than the one in her chest, something hard and huge in her belly, something that says, *This can't happen.*

I can't die yet. I still want—all I want—

Is . . . to . . . to see the Gyre.

Yes.

Just three more days. To know the mycelium made it, and then, Cora swears, *I'll die, I know it, it'll be fine, I'll go without complaint,* and so for the first time Cora listens exactly to what Luis says, stays wrapped in the hammock, drinks Peregrin's bone broth, tries to ignore Peregrin and Luis whispering around her in anxiety, and Cora wishes, hopes, begs.

All I want is three more days.

Two.

One, please, one.

"Cora," Luis calls, and Peregrin says, "Cora, sweetheart, wake up, we're all docked and locked in, I've got your air, let's go," and together they heft her out of the hammock, out of the boat, and she thrashes, violently, but Luis says, "It's alright, Cora, I packed the mycelium up, just like you wrote, they're here, look," and it's true: the trays are stacked and labeled neatly, and now there's someone here, and they're taking the mycelium, legs wide and careful to keep balance because, yes, they're all on a bridge, which is floating on the water, swaying gently. All around her are lights, and boats, rising and shining in the night.

She made it.

This is it.

I got it, everything I wanted.

I can—finally I can—

But peace, a comforting blanket of triumph and private fulfillment she always imagined, doesn't come. Instead her lungs are burning, and her body is heaving. People are around her, lifting her up, and she hears Luis's voice, "Please, Cora, *please,* hang in there," and somehow her feet move beneath her, bringing her forward, forward, with some wild animal hope, as if there might really be someplace left still for her to go, and that place turns out to be a boat heady with the smell of sanitizer. Cora gasps hideously as she is released into a cot; Luis grips her hand as someone approaches, a nurse, maybe, with a stethoscope, and Cora inhales, and inhales, and inhales, ineffectually, and knows, suddenly, that this is really, actually it. Her final moments will be spent like this, in pain, in furious misery and marrow longing and nothing at all of being *glad that she did something useful with her life*. Somewhere in the burning of her body, her mind is even hotter, incendiary.

I want—all I want—is—

Not just one more day.

She wants days, months, years, more, everything: her whole life, all the years she should have had left, stolen from her because she was cheaper than the unspeakable complexities of a corporation cleaning up after itself. Their extravagance stole her hometown, her body, and her future, and left her not even this last minute on earth that she could spend in anything other than excruciation.

The nurse grips Cora's shoulders.

"You're having a panic attack," they say. Their voice is firm: "Close your eyes. Listen. Breathe with me, using your diaphragm, right here," and Cora almost tries to use her precious little wisp of air to shout, *You don't know what you're talking about,* but she sees it now, finally, in the blur of her tears, the nurse's nasal cannula, and her tank, too, and Cora mashes her palms against her eyes, aligns her breathing to the nurse's slow count: *inoutinoutin* . . . *out* . . . *in* . . . out.

"See?" the nurse says, smiling warmly, and Cora—*inhales.* Deeply—fully. She trembles, not from exhaustion now, or cold, but startled awe. As the world starts to re-align around her, she spots Luis, and gapes.

"Look," she gasps, purely from disbelief, and Luis says, "No. *You* look."

"At what?" Cora asks. She looks at the nurse, at the faces of the others in the room, coming into focus again, all staring, at her. Peregrin is covering her mouth. Cora looks down, and notices it, finally, under her collar. Trembling, she rips off her shawl, her sweater, her shirt.

Her skin is glowing. Threading through her palm, her forearm, and up across her entire chest is a lacework of vivid, fervent violet.

Nadine Aurora Tabing is a writer, designer, artist, and shiba inu enthusiast who lives in the Pacific Northwest. Her writing has appeared in *Strange Horizons*. She can be found on Twitter at @suchnadine, and otherwise at nadinetabing.com.

Lies You've Told About the Pacific Garbage Patch

Emily Alta Hockaday

The trash patch did not break us up. The trash patch (or vortex, I should say; it isn't stationary, it is not an island) did not poison the way I look at you or turn your words to stinging flies. We did not get physical; we did not even throw anything. There is a whole toxic ecosystem built around the microscopic plastic particles—a spread of microorganisms feed on the waste. You live on the other side of the gulf. One potential lie is that the bacteria clean it up. One potential lie is that they spread the poisons. One definite lie is that the trash patch is okay. When the medical examiner cuts me open, my stomach will be full of soda rings, plastic threads, and shopping bags, and I will have starved to death. I don't want to spread the poison. Let the mess stop here with me and you. It is time to call it. One lie about the pacific garbage patch is that it is the only garbage patch in our oceans. It is not. At 5,000 square kilometers, it is simply the biggest.

Emily Hockaday is a poet and editor living in Queens. Her first full-length collection, *Naming the Ghost*, debuted with Cornerstone Press in 2022. She is the author of the poetry chapbooks *Starting a Life*, *What We Love & Will Not Give Up*, *Ophelia: A Botanist's Guide*, and *Space on Earth*. Her poems have appeared in print and online journals, as well as with the *Poets of Queens* and *Parks & Points' Wayfinding* anthologies. Emily is the recipient of a New York City Artists Corps grant, a Café Royal Cultural Foundation grant, and the winner of the Middle House Review Editors' Prize. Her poems have been featured on RadioLab, with the performance series Emotive Fruition, and in the Office Hours Fellows showcase events. You can find Emily on the web at www.emilyhockaday.com or @E_Hockaday.

Why We Bury Our Dead at Sea

Tehnuka

"Does the defendant admit posting this message after the sinking of the ship *Deep Power*?" The prosecution lawyer looked up from his papers, directly at Kaveri. "I quote: 'A hundred oilers nowhere near make up for even a single whale fall, but I guess it's a start, el-oh-el'."

My cousin, blank-faced in the dock, said, "Yes."

The tight bun she'd made of her plaited hair was coming undone. I wanted to go to her and re-tie it. I gripped my thighs with aching fingers and waited.

It wasn't truly an oil ship—I don't know if any ultra-deepwater drilling ships still operate—but trawling for rare earth elements was hardly different, in her mind.

I was scared they'd ask if she believed what she wrote.

Instead, the lawyer said, "Can you elaborate on your meaning?" He must have been hired locally by the company. I can't distinguish subtle regional variations, but knew his accent was a New Zealand one.

"Entire deep sea ecosystems were created and thrived on the nutrition from dead whales that sank to the seafloor, but in the absence of whales, I guess humans will do."

The judge frowned.

No one I care about was particularly sad when the *Deep Power* sank. So much we loved was already lost beneath the sea—we had no sympathy to spare. But all of us, except Kaveri, had kept those thoughts to ourselves.

She looked thinner, as worn as her patched-up secondhand clothes, standing there alone. Her friends hadn't come to support her. I didn't blame them. We knew as soon as she was questioned that this would, at the very least, jeopardise her—our—climate residency. Then, the previous month, her charges were read out in this same courtroom—a rearranged hall in the International Seabed Authority's local premises. The list started with something like 'anti-green energy propaganda' and ended with blowing a hole in a ship carrying ninety-seven crew members. No one wanted to risk being associated with that.

A little money did quietly appear in our bank account, enough to talk to a lawyer. They told me it was Kaveri's bad luck that the ship hadn't sunk in Aotearoa waters; the International Seabed Authority had its own way of handling trials, and national courts wouldn't want to touch this case. I'd be permitted to attest to Kaveri's good character if called as a witness, but unless they found new fragmented evidence six thousand metres underwater to prove she was involved, the outcome would largely depend on a judge's assessment of her social media statements.

The company representative, when his turn came, spent a long minute staring at his papers. He addressed the entire courtroom, eyes darting often towards the lone reporter and their camera. "We have a chance to break free from petroleum—from a world dependent on burning the carcasses of millions-of-years-dead organisms to pollute the air—and to avert future wars centred on the resources of vulnerable nations already devastated by the effects of climate change." He held his hands out, palms up, and lowered his voice. "The seafloor is common property; we could all be richer for sharing its wealth. *Deep Power*, and its crew, stood for that promise. We all believed the time of conflict minerals was past. And now, these . . . eco-terrorists have devastated that—"

He was cut off by the judge, who reminded him that no eco-terrorism had yet been proven.

I wondered if others in the courtroom saw through his evangelism, or if I was the only one on Kaveri's side.

An old neighbour rows me back to the house, anchoring upriver at the rusted post that used to be a front gate. He says he'll be back in a few hours and leaves me to pick through the remnants of our long-lost lives.

The blue-inked label on the cassette is an illegible smudge. Even if it hadn't been water damaged, we must have re-recorded over it dozens of times. Nevertheless, it takes me back twenty years to that morning when I stood beneath screeching gulls, nose wrinkled as I pressed buttons at random on the video camera inherited from our great-grandmother.

That memory is so clear. It cools my heart to find something that cuts through the blur of the trial last month—the thin grey carpet, pens tapping against polished-wood tables, and stuffy summer air.

We'd collected the camera the day before, from the antique shop that repaired it and found us an old tape. My little cousin was determined to film her own documentary for school and apparently my new cellphone was an environmental travesty.

"Can we do this quickly? It stinks like rotting sewage!"

"It's RICH NUTRIENTS that go into the OCEAN," Kaveri replied. "Anyway, I'm ready. It's you that should hurry up."

"If only Chinnamma and Chiththappa had named you for a deity instead of this damned river, we might be singing at the temple right now!"

She danced barefoot, between lumpy tree-roots that bent upwards seeking air through mud. Waggled thin fingers overhead, as if to mimic their reach. "There's a red light when you start recording."

I finally found it.

She put on her best television voice. She'd been watching old clips of some famous British naturalist. "These ancient mangroves may not seem much at first glance, but—"

Her next words were about carbon fixing and nutrients flushed into the coastal ocean. The beauty of the mangroves. I noticed that her leggings were covered in mud, and somehow she'd managed to smear it on her hair. I contemplated how to prevent her dirtying the car: whether we should just leave it there and trek home through the muck, or find clean water to rinse off. I thought of how we could have gone to a zoo to film lions from a pristine concrete walkway, or visited beautiful plants in the botanical gardens full of fragrances that aimed to please the human nose. By the time we'd found crabs and oysters, or whatever she was looking for, and she'd told the camera how mangroves slowed climate change and protected us from storm surges, gloopy sediment clung to my legs too, and we had run out of tape.

"Ah well, the marks are just for the essay," she said, trailing a toe through silt sodden with the rising tide. I wondered why she'd needed me at all, but only briefly. The smell had faded into the background as we searched for animal tracks and flicked through her plant book, and I overflowed with love for her, and the joys she always introduced me to.

"Ivvalavumthana?" says the neighbour, studying the plastic cassette in my hand. He scuffs bare feet through what used to be our garden. "Isn't there anything else?"

We both look downhill at the boat. I always hoped we would return, once I'd saved enough for the voyage, thinking we'd benefit from closure after the way we fled during the worst of the storms. I should be grateful to find anything left here to say a proper farewell to. But seeing the house only reminds me I've lost two homes now.

I shake my head. "Found everything salvageable. Some knick-knacks upstairs." I tap the suitcase beside me. "Old books."

Not the photo albums, the letters, the remnants of my family. Not her.

I keep clutching the tape.

The smell from that day down in the mangroves seems to have suffused the air here too, although nowadays it could well be from rotting sewage. Still, when I inhale, it brings with it the recollection of something else Kaveri said: "Mangroves are the lungs of the ocean." She breathes so much life into this world.

I think of those roots straining for oxygen above the incoming tide. When the waters recede, what's left are memories, coated in sediment and bad smells. The richness is always washed into the sea.

At Kaveri's questioning, she said whatever came to mind, as she always had.

She talked about her work. Yes, they had seen the *Deep Power* and yes, she had gone for a dive nearby because she'd never seen a deep-sea miner before and yes, she was an environmentalist or she wouldn't be volunteering to reseed coral reefs while her cousin paid the bills, would she? The prosecution lawyer asked what she knew about deep-sea mining. She talked about creatures that grew on metallic nodules that grew in the depths of the ocean. About noises and echolocation and plumes of sediment that clouded the water for kilometres. About how everything that happened on this planet was connected.

"I didn't know the ship that sank was the same one I saw until I was ordered to come in for questioning."

The lawyer pursed his lips before asking what I'd dreaded. Did she believe what she had written?

She folded her arms. For the first time, her voice quivered. "If things had been different, we could have still had whales."

When I was sworn in, the judge kept telling me to talk louder. The sound sank into the humidity. It reminded me of early days here, when people kept telling me to speak up or repeat myself, correcting the way I pronounced words I'd known my whole life.

I told the court how our family had raised my cousin to care about everyone around her.

"So you agree she has a single-minded focus on wildlife preservation?"

"No, not wildlife—humans too. We're not separate. There's no 'them' and 'us'," I said, hands clasped tight. This couldn't be helping her case. "Kaveri said it already. We're part of the same ecosystem. It's better for everyone when it's in balance."

She looked up at me then, eyes bright.

I told them about the river she was named for and its delta in which we grew up; the city lost to the sea centuries ago; the family we lost in the storms. "Kaveri knows loss. She wouldn't inflict it on anyone. Even when she was a little kid, she just wanted to show the world the beauty of what was left. She used to have me film her own documentaries.... I wish I could show you. I had them on my phone but everything's gone. When we came here, we had nothing except my job offer." My shoulders ached. I seemed to have swallowed a whole lot of air, making my stomach churn. "And Kaveri wouldn't have knowingly put our residency application at risk either. She made a thoughtless comment, and maybe she doesn't understand how it looks, but she didn't mean to hurt anyone, and she definitely had nothing to do with the ship sinking."

She gazed fixedly past me at the white-painted walls.

Now everyone knew who I was, I sat at the back of the public gallery, as far as possible from relatives and friends of the crew. The reporter, adjusting their camera, was the only person with a smile for me; Kaveri didn't turn back in my direction. And, in the end, my attempt to emphasise her naivete made little difference.

"I didn't do it," she said. "And I don't celebrate death; I only celebrate that it happened where it did. The oceans we came from are our mother. We have taken life from her and left her starving, we've made it impossible for our siblings to live. I hope eventually we will crawl into the oceans, and re-evolve to replace what we stole. But since this cannot happen for millennia, and since this is all we can do now, why not celebrate any chance to give back? When I die, I want my body to feed the abyssal depths. Bury me in the sea, too."

She was sent back to her cell and they wouldn't let me talk to her. They said judgement was reserved. It could be months before a verdict. I had to take the train back up north to wait for news.

Our residency application was declined a week later.

That night, the wind blew strong and the bay glimmered in blue light. A crowd stretched along the sand flats, well after midnight, taking photos. I left off packing to join them. It seemed a good omen: microscopic life, thriving. A respite from my despair.

Several hundred long-finned pilot whales—Kaveri would remind me they're dolphins, really—stranded in the morning, the deep red tide of the water that brought them mirroring the brightness of pōhutukawa blossom against dark leaves and blue sky.

We cooled them with towels soaked in toxic seawater, into which we'd refloat survivors when the tide returned.

Sea-salt and sweat-salt stuck to our t-shirts. Others took breaks to lather on sunscreen. The waves lapped higher.

As our dolphin gave a weak tail-flick, the person working beside me said, "I wish we could have helped. If nothing else, maybe they'll fall to the seafloor?"

"I was thinking the same. My cousin said. . . ."

"We've got it from here," said a rescue officer, approaching. "Thanks."

The two of us turned to wade back.

"You're Kaveri's cousin, eh?"

"Were you at the trial?" I stopped, a low wave sloshing at my shins.

“My friend sent me the last video.” They splashed up next to me, pushing cracked sunglasses onto their forehead. “He’s been on her side from the start. I’m sorry, must be rough waiting. Though . . . she’s right, isn’t she? About giving back?”

Unwilling to dump the ruined tape, I take it back to where I’m staying, in the spare room of a stranger’s house near the Kaveri River delta. Here, I eke out what remains of our savings, seeking work that might offer me a visa back to Aotearoa. This is a new kind of loneliness—albeit an incomplete one, because every day, I receive more messages:

“I saw her testimony. I’m writing it in my will.”

“My sister runs a charter boat company and found a funeral director to team up with. They’re booked solid.”

“I’d like to interview you about Kaveri’s trial.”

“I’ve been sending that court video to everyone I know, it’s incredible.”

“Would you be able to put us in touch with your cousin?”

I can’t, because Kaveri is languishing in custody still waiting for the verdict. In the meantime, the company has launched a new forensic investigation.

But now, out here—all over the planet—we bury our dead at sea.

Tehnuka (she/they) is a writer and volcanologist from Aotearoa New Zealand. She likes to find herself up volcanoes, down caves, and in unexpected places; everyone else, however, can find her online at www.tehnuka.dreamhosters.com or as @tehnuka on Twitter, and some of her stories in the Imagine 2200 climate fiction collection, *Worlds of Possibility*, and *If There's Anyone Left.*

After encountering the grey whales in El Burbujon, Laguna Ojo de Liebre

Naila Francis

When I say I miss being with the whales,
what I mean is sitting on the panga
in a lagoon in the blue middle of nowhere.

Nothing to do but be this body,
let the other bodies come, rise
from stillness to rest beneath my palm,
the ache to take up space—

live as exclamation,
breach-bloomed in this world.

When I say I miss being with the whales,
I want water
the holiest kind of love.

What I mean is my mother carried me
into the sea, her round belly, joyful
breath giving my lungs their rhythm,
my first cry of grief
to feel myself,
an underwater creature, released
to sudden cold.

When I say I miss being with the whales,
what I mean is, who wouldn't rather rhapsody
than longing, want the place that dreamed
them wild than the weight of the return.

Listen, some praises are ineffable.

And I may be the mermaid I say I am.

But I-less are the words
that bend us to all we cherish,
what we must bless and save.

Naila Francis is a writer, grief doula and wedding officiant based in Philadelphia. She is also a founding member of Salt Trails, an interdisciplinary collective honoring grief through community rituals. Her poetry has previously been published in *North of Oxford*, *Scribbler*, *Voicemail Poems* and the Healing Verse Poetry Line.

A Predatory Transience

C. G. Aubrey

This is your reservation reminder from Palmetto Kayak Adventure Tours. Your four-hour self-guided tour is scheduled for today, 1–5pm. Reply 1 to confirm, 2 to cancel. Hope to see you soon!

The text is waiting when I wake up. White letters stark against the black text box. I don't bother looking at the number. I've made no such reservation, nor the one for Lowcountry Marsh Tours that I was sent on last year, or Saltmarsh Wanderings the year before that. The origin of the texts remains untraceable, and I've had some smart people looking.

The first time, I thought I'd won a giveaway. I like to ramble down to Charleston and the Sea Islands a few times a year, spend half a day out on the water laughing with the gulls and crying in wonder at the rays and dolphins. A giveaway wasn't too far-fetched. It wasn't until I got where I was going that I knew why I was there. Now it's an affirmation of faith, a call and response between me and the sea.

I text back to confirm and dress for the day. Water leggings, sports bra, and a long-sleeved sun shirt; baseball cap from a school in the northern part of the state. I'm what they call a local tourist, not quite a local, definitely not one of the out-of-state offenses the Sun Belt is forced to rely upon for revenue. Still, it's an hour drive down to Folly Island and I have time to sit in the quiet truck and talk to myself, make sure this is what I want to do. What I *still* want to do. It's not new to me. Ten years since that first text and I've taken over a dozen of these impromptu trips, trusting that I'm doing my small part to leave the marsh—maybe the world—better than I found it.

My friends marvel at my impulsiveness. My bravery. My *joie de vivre*. They can't imagine going anywhere on their own, much less out onto the water, but I'm rarely more than a few hundred yards from shore and 80% of the water I'm on isn't even over my head. It's not like I'm out free climbing red rocks without a safety partner.

"Ms. McDonald?"

I'm never what they're expecting and today less so. It's a perfect November day and the weather is beautiful—bright blue sky, sun blade-sharp as it glints off the dark water—but there's a storm off the coast and the breeze is fierce. I'll be paddling into a 15mph wind and spend most of the paddle out against the tide. I don't look like the athletic type.

Whatever that's supposed to mean.

"Like the farmer," I confirm with a very realistic moo-moo here. Sometimes the joke lands, sometimes it doesn't, but the couple behind the counter is closer to my age, granola crunchy sapphics from the upstate who made their way south in the nineties and found Charleston more hospitable. Angela's name tag boasts a rainbow flag pin not too different than the one she's just noticed on my hat. She grins back and I add, "That's me."

"Gonna be a rough afternoon out there," she warns, but she takes my credit card anyway. "But if you stick to the edges, you'll be alright. Should be able to get a little paddling in before the wind gets worse."

I've paid for four hours. I'm not coming in until it's storming or dark, but I'm used to people underestimating me. When I was younger, when I had more to prove, it used to infuriate me. Somewhere around thirty, I realized it was a gift. By the time I turned forty, it was a miracle.

No one expects much of a round, middle-aged white woman. They suspect her even less.

Angela and I make small talk as I sign the necessary waivers and give them my emergency contacts. Her wife, Kathy, tells me to be careful. They seem a little reluctant to send me out until I show them my waterproof phone in its floaty bag. They ask if I have water and I show them my favorite insulated steel flask. It's so big it has its own sling across my back and holds enough water for most of the day. If I have to I can use it as a bludgeoning weapon.

They don't need to know that last part.

"There's an old boat they beached on this little creek," Angie says, handing me a laminated map of the King Flats Creek and its tiny tributaries. Some of the brackish waterways are so small they only really exist at high tide. "It's full of crabs."

"I'll be sure to check it out."

It's all very up and up. They give me back my card and I head out to the landing. The salt in the air is holy, by day's end I'll be dusted and glittering like a sea pixie, anointed.

The Folly kid waiting with my bright red kayak is too young to be a burned-out hippy, but he's burned out just the same. A full-time resident of the island, with long, salt-dried, sun-bleached hair that might have once been brown, skin burned and bronzed like the bottom of a biscuit. I couldn't guess at his age; his face and hands are weathered from outdoor life. What brain cells he has left know more about the tides and marsh than I ever will.

But it doesn't call to him.

"You're a local right?" he asks, hope drawing a frown between his warm, brown eyes.

"Local tourist," I admit with a smile that always disarms. "From swamp country, an hour or so north."

We have our own tourist problem, though it's migratory. Every spring, they come for the lakes and the golf-course weather. If there's a polo-shirt, cleat-wearing version of me wildflower-bombing thousands of acres of pesticide-soaked bentgrass, I don't need to know about it, but I wish her well.

"Ah." Folly kid nods in almost approval, like he knows a little of what I'm thinking. Maybe he does. He takes a deep breath and I find myself inhaling with him, a slow toke of pungent pluff mud air. "Bit different down here."

He likes me, feels safe around me just like most wild creatures. He smells a little sweet, like good pot and seawater. Nothing worse to him than the necessary evil of tourists.

"It is," I agree. "But it's nice to get out on someone else's water every now and then."

I'm not arrogant enough to think myself at home here. This isn't my land. It's not even the land of my people. Some of my people stole it from the Kussoe centuries ago. I'm an interloper. An occasional predator necessary to the ecosystem, but neither resident nor invasive.

He nods again, sagely, points with his chin at the rough, rippling water. "Too salty here for snakes or alligators."

It's mostly true. They're what biologists call transient species. Animals who only spend part of their lives in the marsh. Alligators are as rare as I am; the daily commuters are dolphins, rays, and small sharks. Each drawn into the intertidal area by the promise of calm water and good hunting.

Local tourists, like me.

"It'll be a little rough getting across," he says. He's worried about the currents too. The river is wide here, a dark reflection of autumn sky. Clouds may gather like omens a few miles southeast, but the way the weather wavers, it's unlikely I'll see rain.

I zip on my life vest just to make him feel better and assure him that I have been kayaking before. He gives me the same speech he gives everyone, marks a couple of points of interest on the map with a wet fingertip, including the crab boat.

"Just stick to the edge," he says, finally. "Tide'll be with you on the way back, make the return a whole lot easier."

He pushes my boat half out into the water, and waits for me to get settled. I take my time, storing my water bottle out of the way, clipping my floaty-bag to a bungee by my seat. I have a multi-tool in my waist pouch and a mesh bag for litter. There's always something out there that shouldn't be.

"Ready?"

It's been a rough two years, pandemic and all that, and this is my first trip beyond my own swamp in eighteen months. I brace myself, mentally and physically, for the send-off. I'm not a small woman, and part of me still expects to be too big, too heavy for something as simple and finite as the laws of buoyancy. I don't know why—except cultural conditioning—it's not like I'm close to the kayak's weight limit, but it's hard being a woman who takes up space.

Fat. I know we're supposed to be reclaiming that word, giving it the neutral value it's supposed to have, but it's never been neutral to me. Maybe if I were a whale or a seal or a manatee. Maybe if fat was something you had instead of something you are.

I tug on my gloves and pick up my paddle. "Ready."

On the water, I'm just another round marine creature. I'm heavy, but I'm strong. My body has never failed to do what I want or need it to. That's all the water cares about. If it cares at all. Bigger and stronger than I get lost beneath its surface every day. Having come back from drowning twice as a child, I'm acutely aware of this. I still get a cold skitter down my spine whenever I cross deep, dark water. Doesn't matter how many times I manage it safely.

There's only one wrong breath between us and oblivion.

The Folly kid was right; it's rough crossing the widest part of the river. It's deep water, permanent. I look both ways before I start to cross, a mostly useless habit out here. The big boats stick to the center, and most run a low wake, but not all. It's not like a kayaker is fast enough to get out of the way. We rely on common courtesy, the laws—both written and not—of water etiquette.

Across the water, miles of *Spartina* grass wave, green and gilded and filled with the surf-sounding tumble of a brisk sea wind. The water along the edge is calm as promised, and I'm halfway across when an offshore fishing boat goes zipping by too fast. Post-911 country music blares, louder than the breeze, and the tattered nylon buzz of an American flag hangs past respectful retirement on the *Master Baiter's* stern. I raise my paddle and let the waves push me roughly toward the bank. Assholes. Serve them right if it's them that I'm here for, but there's no use worrying about that yet.

The kayak bottoms out, a soft bump then a harsh grate as the tough plastic scrapes against oyster shells clustered in the shallows. I wait for the water to calm again, for the smell of diesel exhaust to sweep past me and vanish, before I push back off, paddle digging into the muddy bank. A handful of long-legged oystercatchers dash along beside me, footprints disappearing in the damp sand, bright red bills flashing amid grey-shelled oysters. They're not bothered by the assholes; maybe I shouldn't be either.

Not yet.

My paddling form is terrible, clunky. Doesn't matter how often I come. My arms are short or I'm clumsy. Maybe both. I don't know. I just know practice hasn't cured me. But the wildlife never seems to mind. I know it's partly because they're accustomed to worse than me, but I like to think they know I'm no threat to them, that they welcome me among them. I paddle ahead of the birds and grab my phone, snap photos as the wind pushes me back. A scoop of pelicans swoop low in front of me and I get their pictures as well before I lose too much momentum. Then it's back to balancing, staying close enough to the bank that I don't have to fight the wind, but not so close that I'm bottoming out every dozen yards.

I might not be getting my steps in, but I'm getting my workout. At least I'm not sweaty. Soaked through from wind and sub-par paddling form, but not sweaty. I love being out here.

Surrounded by water, sky, and marsh. The entire day is blue-white and golden, a perfect mid-seventies. Overhead a red-tailed hawk circles. Tiny birds dart through the cordgrass, marsh wrens and salt-marsh sparrows, nibbling on grass seeds and insects.

Every time I check my map or stop for water, I drift back. I've kayaked before but nothing like this. The marsh is usually peaceful as a warm bath, and I've never really bemoaned my poor paddling form, but I'm regretting it today, even as I'm grateful to have remembered my gloves. My first time out I went home with blisters and that was on water as smooth as glass.

The grass opens up on my left, the small tributary with the promised crab boat. It's not quite the halfway point of my four hours, but I'm tired enough to take the respite. The wind doesn't roar here, it sighs, and so do I, letting as much of the last year go as I can. I take a selfie with a great blue heron who seems utterly unconcerned with my presence, post it and a few other pictures to the 'gram. Establishing a timeline. An alibi.

Perfect fall day on the water!

As promised, just around a bend, a derelict fishing boat has been overturned and run aground. Repurposed as a crab habitat, its sun-scoured, barnacle-covered surface swarms with orange-fisted fiddler crabs, claws raised in warning as my shadow falls too close. I salute the intrepid arthropods and paddle past, bank my kayak and take a few more photos, then a water break in the quiet. The sun is nap-warm and my arms are just starting to get tired. I toy with the idea of hiding here for what little is left of the afternoon, but there's work waiting for me.

A chip wrapper flashes silver from the bank. Beside it lies a plastic milk jug and a tangled knot of fishing line the size of my fist. The fishing line is the worst, but that silver flashes like a lure to more than me out here. I use my paddle to drag the rubbish to the edge of my kayak, throw one leg off the other side to balance as I lean down to pick it up. The water's cold this late in the season, and even knowing the bottom is only inches beneath my dangling foot, I feel the silty truth of my own vulnerability. I distract myself with a few curses for all litterbugs and head back out.

The tide turns as I reach the widest part of the creek. It's deep water here, and the storm current is strong, pushing me back the way I've come even as the leaving tide pulls me forward. I fight along with the water, because it's not in me not to, because there is a single crystalline moment when it's just me and the water and the wind and I am both insignificantly small and cosmically stubborn. Immortal, ephemeral. My entire being surrendering to the frantic pursuit of perseverance, ultimately going nowhere.

I hate it, but I am still paddling.

I have a moment to doubt, a moment to wonder if the marsh really chose me or if my descent into madness was the inevitable product of growing up in a late-stage capitalist hellscape, consuming too many Disney Princess movies and 90s environmentalist cartoons. What makes me any different than the white kids deep-diving into far-right radicalism on Youtube?

An hour before sunset, the marsh grass shadows stretch long, dark reflections in the unquiet water. The Atlantic is just a song away; the salt in the air thickens. Last time I was here, my sister and I turned back about a quarter-mile before King Flats merges with Folly and Oak Island creeks, but I've never been this far out alone. A pair of osprey crisscross above me, hunting cries all but lost in the wind, and even though I'm expecting them, I startle when the first bonnethead shark bumps the bottom of my boat.

"You're late," I accuse, as if there is any timeline but that of the marsh.

The second little shark swipes the side of my kayak, movements reminiscent of herding dogs. Soon there are a dozen swimming close to the surface, avoiding my paddle with enviable agility. Bonnethead sharks aren't big enough to threaten people, even if they wanted to, which they don't. They're the smallest of the hammerheads—in hammer and in length—tending around three to four feet long and traveling in schools of twelve to fifteen. Omnivores, if you can imagine. They're the only sharks we know of whose diet consists equally of plants. They forage into the marsh because they like swimming along the bottom of shallow water, grazing on sea lettuce and crustaceans.

I take a deep breath, my doubts sinking to the bottom like so much detritus. It won't be long now. Longest it's ever taken from pick up to target is ten minutes. I lift my paddle from the water and let the bonnetheads bump and nudge and push the nose of my kayak in the direction they want me going. Nothing about my escort is natural. They're not false-smiling bottle-nosed dolphins charming boaters with swim-bys and strand feedings.

Whatever time is left, I spend preparing: turning off my phone, making sure it's safely secured in the kayak. I take a few gulps of water. No matter how often we do this my throat always gets dry. My shirt is salt-crusted, lips wind-chapped. I'd be sunburned if I didn't insist on an unreasonable SPF. I check the fit of my gloves, flex salt from the creases. My arms feel like jelly and my feet have pressed to the pegs for so long, I can't tell what my legs are doing. That's pretty normal, especially after a long time sitting in the boat. When I finally get back to the landing, Folly kid will tell me to go slow getting up and he'll hover, not wanting a customer to land on their ass.

A curved fin breaks the water beside me, and my heart leaps free of its fears as a pair of dolphins breach gently, grey sides slick with watercolor sunset. They cross in front of my kayak and then something heavier than a bonnethead bumps beneath my seat. What makes me different from those radicalized kids? They do. An unnatural alliance. Sharks, dolphins, and the raptors overhead. Disparate species gathering together, water and wildlife willing me on their way.

Whatever my reluctance, it's lost in exaltation. We make the last deep bend of King Flats Creek. Ahead is Folly Creek, then a half-mile farther the Atlantic. The *Master Baiter* is anchored in the confluence of the three creeks, and yes, I'm glad it's them. The water is dark, filled with the sky's reflection, but there's something floating like oil just below all that sky. As I draw closer to the boat, I can see that it's blood.

It's legal to chum in South Carolina; it's a standard fishing practice. There are certain restrictions around certain beaches, but I've never bothered learning them. I don't care about what's legal, I only care about what's right. Here, in this quiet sanctuary, it is defilement. Sacrilege. I pick up my paddle, stick one end forward on my right and cut hard to port.

They're "shark fishing." The kind of nonsense that leaves hooks in mouths and bullet wound scars on heads, backs, and sides. We're supposed to leave nothing behind, but some people think that the only way to be remembered is to leave a scar upon the earth.

They're always the same. White men with too much or too little money. Ignorant of all but their own entitlement. I don't need to have the first fin brought to my attention, but whatever brought me out here wants to be sure of my investment, I guess. One of the dolphins swims up alongside, eye lifted out of the water, a dark certainty in the meeting of our gaze. The fin in her mouth is small, cut clean, not torn or ripped like any non-human might manage.

The *Master Baiter* looms with laughter and loud music. Three figures move along the deck, but they haven't noticed me. It's impossible to hear the gunshots over the wind, but the creatures around my boat recoil with every shot, and the kayak seems to reverberate with fear and anger and my own trembling rage. When my bow brushes the side of the boat, the sharks and dolphins dive. I don't see the darker shadow that follows, but I can feel it, a low quiet rising from the deep water like a promise.

They're too busy taking turns shooting into the water to notice me. I grab a line and tether my kayak to the ladder on the side of the boat. By the time they realize they're not alone, I'm onboard, leaning back against the rail, situation and targets assessed.

Early twenties. Gym muscles and soft hands. Beach blonde hair growing out from hundred-dollar haircuts. Perfect teeth, expensive sunglasses. They're not kids; they're grown-ass men languishing too long under the protective banner of boys. Their parents have summer homes in places like Beaufort and Isle of Palms and Frogmore Isle, but they like to come to the marshes and cosplay the local rednecks in cut-up Dirty Crab t-shirts of buxom cartoon girls covered in double entendres.

"I called ahoy," I lie with a nod back to my kayak. The boat smells like beer and blood and fish guts and there's a red, white, and jingoist anthem twanging from the stereo. I can't hear what they're saying, but cruelty has its own cadence. There's no doubt about why I'm here. "Water was getting rough. Y'all mind if I tie up for a few minutes, get my second wind?"

They glance back and forth between each other. The one holding the gun—it's a 9mm Glock; I can't even—tucks it into the back waistband of jeans he bought already ripped to hell.

"Naw." His accent is bad, either a part of the south I'm not from or something he picked up on those faux southern reality shows, the ones that wouldn't know a real southern accent if it blessed their fucking hearts. "We're just doing a little fishing."

He pulls at the brim of his trucker hat. I can't tell if he's trying to tip it at me politely or if he's just nervous. I can't see his eyes, but I don't need to. He realizes he's caught. He just doesn't know what net he's in.

"Water's rough for fishing," I say as his buddies fall back to flank him. They're just out of arm's reach, but that's okay. I've nearly got my legs back.

The other two aren't nervous. They've done nothing wrong and they're used to being the most important people in any given room. The guy with the gun, well, he's a little squirmy, wondering how much I saw, how much trouble I can get him in. He's been in trouble for stupid shit before. I don't know this for certain, but I recognize the type. Daddy's important or wants to be; Junior keeps costing him money and reputation with the cover-ups.

"S'posed to calm down this evening," says one of Junior's buddies. He's got blood and offal on the hem of his t-shirt, and I avoid looking at the mess on deck. It's clear they've never cleaned a fish before; they're not fishing for food or even sport. They just want to kill something. "Hoping to get a good haul tonight."

Junior can't decide what to do with his hands. He crosses his arms in front of his chest. Uncrosses them. I don't say anything about the gun; I already know it's mine. Just as soon as he turns his back to me. Whether that's before or after one of his buddies hits the water is all that remains to be seen.

I just want to kill something too.

"Not really the ideal spot for shark fishing," I say lightly. They could shrug it off if they wanted to, but they're not the type to take criticism from a woman who isn't their momma or their unfortunate girlfriend.

"It is if you put enough bait out." Junior laughs, and I decide I'm going to leave him for last.

I don't answer. Instead, I make a show of stretching. When a fat woman does anything active, people tend to look away or stare in judgment. They turn back to the rail, and I'm instantly forgotten as the third one leans too far over, reaching down toward the water.

"Chad, on your right!" Bloody Hem says excitedly.

I get close enough to see that he has a bangstick partially submerged. I've never seen one in action—they're used by divers and spear-fishers as shark deterrents—and I doubt this is anything like the right way, but I've seen the effects of them, photographs of three-inch deep holes in the broad beautiful heads of bull sharks somehow still swimming.

Chad leans farther out, stretching, stretching . . . stretching.

It doesn't take much. The idiot isn't even flat-footed. He's on his toes, leaning out as far as he can and still keep his weapon in the water. His buddies are cheering him on. When he tips face-first into the water, it takes them entirely too long to realize I pushed him. Hell, if I hadn't grabbed Junior's gun—easily, far too easily—they might have kept laughing, assuming Chad was shit-faced enough to lose his balance.

But I have Junior's gun.

"What the fuck, bitch?!"

The violence simmers up on an outraged shout that is always just beneath the surface with these kinds of men. Junior takes a step towards me and I shake my head once. He should be grateful I'm not stuck using my vacuum flask.

"Shh . . . ." I don't know if they can hear me over the wind, over the country music twanging beneath cries of the gathering gulls, but they still, gazes darting to each other like frightened baitfish.

It's been years since I held a handgun. I've always preferred revolvers, at least until the gun nuts ruined that for the rest of us. I have a rifle and a shotgun at home. One for hunting, the other for scaring off coyotes or any other uninviteds too close to my house. The 9mm feels like a toy, but Bloody Hem and Junior are taking me seriously now that I have it leveled at them. I wonder how many bullets are left in the clip.

"You can't steal my boat." Junior has misread the situation.

I can't help but laugh. Confusion reddens their faces.

"I don't want your boat." I make eye contact with Bloody Hem through his polarized shades, point toward the water with the gun, then back at him. "Go on. You can take your chances in the water or don't. But I'ma see how many bullets you have left in three . . . two . . . ."

They stare at me in disbelief, but they jump before I get to one. I'm actually a little surprised, though I shouldn't be. Courage is in short supply among this particular demographic. They don't know what to do when they aren't the ones holding the gun.

Twin splashes quickly become desperate thrashing. Just off the bow, the water writhes and churns with blood and unidentifiable voids. When I see a terrified face too close to the surface, I lean out and down, close enough that skill hardly matters. Close enough that the Glock could have been a bangstick. I put a bullet between Chad's wide blue eyes. Now he's bait. If there's an afterlife or a next life or purgatory, maybe someone can teach him about irony and just deserts.

Bloody Hem screams something watery and incoherent, but he's no fool. He's swimming hard for the ladder at the boat's stern. He doesn't see the unnaturally large bull shark gliding behind him, Junior's arm hanging out one side of her beautiful mouth.

But I do.

She's not a real shark. With very rare exceptions, even the biggest and hungriest sharks want little to do with us. She's something else, both more and less than the reality of a bull shark. She's vengeance and requiem, the physical manifestation of the marsh's need.

Junior surfaces behind her with a scream, his remaining hand clutching the bloody stump of his arm. Bloody Hem looks back and sees... well, he's not sure what he sees. He's not the kind to recognize his own end, but I make sure Junior sees me raise the gun. His buddy falls back, eyes round and mouth gaping, blood spreading bright across Dirty Crab's Bait Shack.

Junior doesn't suffer nearly as long as I want him to, but I need to head home. I put the last bullet in his back and toss the gun overboard. When the scavengers come to feast, I slip down the ladder, feet just above the autumn sea, waiting. The bonnetheads and dolphins return, the little sharks feasting on the small bits of fresh bait. There's a flash of metal at the corner of one gaping mouth, impossible to ignore. I slip out of my life jacket and into the bloody water. It's chilly, not enough to be dangerous, but it's not a pleasant swim. The earth is warming and so the waters are cooling from polar icecap melt. Another month and the bonnetheads may well be swimming south to warmer waters. It's now or spring, if I even see the same ones again.

I'm never sure; I don't always join them. Baiting is bad, even for the best reasons, like data collecting and scientific observation and what I'm doing now: pulling hooks out of lips and fishing lines off of tails with my multi-tool. The last thing wild creatures need is to get too accustomed to humans, but the reality is, they're already tangling with us on the regular. Doing nothing feels like violence.

I tug loose one last hook from the mouth of a large female, fumble my multi-tool back into my pack with cold fingers and the jerky movements of prey that she's polite enough to ignore. When I'm done, she glides around me, silking past me like a cat. Once, twice, three times. She presses her head up against my empty hand, shark-skin benediction scratching lightly at my glove. I would linger if I could, but this is her home, not mine. Maybe one day I'll be another wild creature and not just their agent, but not today.

I climb back out and into my kayak, teeth chattering and shivering in the breeze. The dolphins bump me away, escort me through water painted mango-bright with Lowcountry sunset. Is that water-color reflection stained brighter red than the clouds? I can't say, but it feels like it should be. Red skies and warnings and all of that.

When I turn my phone back on, there is a text waiting.

Thank you for adventuring with us today! We hope to see you again, but not soon.

C. G. Aubrey (she/her) is an autistic writer and outdoor enthusiast obsessed with yellow leaves, pluff mud, and em-dashes. Born and raised in South Carolina, she now lives in eastern North Carolina with the love of her life and too many houseplants. She holds dual-masters degrees in US History and Religious Studies and is currently working on *The Danziger Forgeries*, a queer-norm fantasy/eco-horror with vengeful trees and sharp-toothed marsh ponies. When she's not writing or lost in research, she is probably kayaking or taking too many selfies with local trees. Find her on Instagram @c.g.aubrey and www.cgaubrey.com.

Facebook Event: Run into the Category 5 Winds of a Woman Pretending to be a Hurricane

Anastasia Jill

Line up your cars, drive to the storm post-evacuation
 7 pm. September 10th. The Keys.

Grab your guitar and serenade the hurricane with Wonderwall
 8 p.m. September 10th. Daytona Beach.

Buy the hurricane a drink; ask if she's from Tennessee.
 9 p.m. September 10th. Miami-Dade.

Give the hurricane your number and ask her for sexts.
 9:15 p.m. Haha, then what? :)

Ask permission to touch her cheekbones, trigger
eye socket replacement, kick sand in her hair when
she says no.
 10 p.m. Location TBD.

Mock her double eyewall, drink laughter like salt water.
 11 p.m. Downtown Orlando, in a building.

Fold her in half, make her an oblong joke, don't take
her serious.
 Midnight. All 67 counties in the state.

Discover her foundations are thicker than your tongue.
Get mad she knows her strength.
 1 a.m. The Panhandle.

Bury mines along the beach. She's just a storm. Who cares?
2:00 a.m. Tampa Bay Area.

She won't feel anything as she tastes rooftops and gets shingles and plywood stuck between her teeth
3:00 a.m. Polk County.

She won't feel anything. A storm's pain doesn't matter.
4:00 a.m. Downtown Tallahassee.

Watch as she writhes on the ground, trying to organize while men in weather coats probe her with cameras.
5:00 a.m. The Calm Before.

Massage her scalp, soft like baby hairs as she digs
her nails into your power lines. She steals all your power
because you've stripped her winds, naked.
! Your event cannot have too many characters !

You refused to be pragmatic then beat the clouds for their destruction.
6:00 a.m. The State Border. All Clear.

Anastasia Jill (she/they) is a queer writer living in the Southeast United States. She has been nominated for *Best American Short Stories*, *Best of the Net*, and several other honors. Her work has been featured with Poets.org, *Pithead Chapel*, *Contemporary Verse 2*, *Minola Review*, *Broken Pencil*, and more.

A River Dance: Cauvery in Crisis

Dheepa R. Maturi

In my childhood, I remember whispering the names under my breath, determined to ward off my family's amusement by pronouncing them precisely: *Tiruchirappalli* and *Thanjavur*, *Dindigul* and *Erode*, *Coimbatore* and *Chidambaram*. These were the cities of my summer vacations, where I visited relatives, temples, and sights throughout the southeastern Indian state of Tamil Nadu.

Occasionally in view as we traveled by car and train was Cauvery, South India's third-largest river, bisecting Tamil Nadu roughly west to east. My father would point out her drying riverbeds and then explain water cycles and drought and the timing of monsoons. After sweltering hours on the road, I wasn't particularly receptive to his facts and figures. Nevertheless, I listened groggily as he reminisced about the Cauvery of his own childhood, her waters ample and clear, and as he worried for her future.

Now, decades later, Cauvery's crisis conditions have accelerated from pressing to dire. With so many Indian cities losing groundwater at an alarming rate—and indeed, predicted to lose it entirely at any moment—their governments increasingly turn to Cauvery's river water, extracting it with pumps, collecting it in tanks, and then transporting it to clamoring crowds.

As groundwater drains, the water table falls below river levels—which means Cauvery now feeds the groundwater, too, like a mother pouring her attention wherever she's called. But as climate change alters monsoon patterns, Cauvery herself is barely fed and never replenished.

As I hear of the worsening droughts, of the increasing desperation and displacement, it's particularly harrowing to learn which cities in the Cauvery basin are approaching Day Zero, when all the taps run dry. Some are those I visited throughout my childhood, the cities where family members live at the front lines.

A wide rectangular room anchored my grandparents' home in the city of Karur and accommodated most household activities, even eating and sleeping. As a child, a major source of my amusement was cartwheeling from one end of this room to the other, where the narrow passage to the kitchen and bathroom commenced.

At that entryway stood a tiny sink with an equally miniscule faucet—everyone's first stop for morning ablutions, specifically, toothbrushing. I still remember my mother's scolding when I accidentally let the water run while brushing, as well my relatives' look of shock at my wanton disregard. I learned that two or three quick fistfuls of water from the tap were considered sufficient for a rinse and eventually mastered those motions. But my irritation—and shame—lingered.

At the time, I didn't consider the possible reasons for the tight management and careful husbanding of household water—I only felt the inconvenience. I struggled to get my long hair fully washed with the allotted two buckets of bath water. Sitting on a short stool, I used a small chombu to pour the water over my head; it took me a week or so to get the knack of maximizing its coverage.

During summers of drought, I sometimes had to draw my bathwater from a storage well at the side of the bathroom. During those droughts, the thick wall of this storage well was lined with larger chombus, used to catch extra water whenever the taps were running. That captured water would be used later for washing clothes or cleaning the household.

Even in a clean and well-maintained home like my grandparents', the stored water containers attracted the dengue-spreading *Aedes* mosquito species, which hospitalized me at age seven. The stored water itself also presented challenges, often tasting a bit strange and even altering the flavor of the food cooked in it.

My grandparents' home was comfortably outfitted by community standards, with an attached groundwater well, some pipes, and a few sinks. Unlike other families, we did not have to fetch water from elsewhere. With attentive management, there was enough with which to cook, wash, and to transport in stainless steel thermoses when we traveled—after, of course, it had been thoroughly boiled, filtered, and cooled.

At a certain point during my summer vacations, one vision sustained me: returning home to America, filling a tall glass with ice, then adding water straight from the tap. I dreamed of that brimming liquid and my first frosty gulp and the sweet taste.

Just a few more weeks, I'd tell myself.

As a child learning Bharath Natyam, a classical dance form native to South India, I was discouraged at times by the notoriously rigorous physical training. I knew, though, if I bided my time, I'd eventually cross the bridge from nritta (physical steps) to nrithya (facial expressions), and finally, to what I longed for: natya (drama). At its heart, Bharath Natyam is a storytelling tradition, and I longed to be the one dancing those stories.

The stories were those I'd learned from my parents and grandparents, from books and Sunday School lessons—compelling tales of sages, warriors, kings. Later, in high school and college, I enjoyed researching these stories further, digging into their philosophical and spiritual dimensions, and then watching as expert dancers communicated those more esoteric aspects.

For example, a physically skilled dancer might accurately execute Shiva's signature tandava dance—but could she demonstrate how it symbolized the ever-pulsing circle of creation and destruction? An expressive dancer might easily portray a woman's assiduous search for her beloved—but could she evoke the soul's longing to merge with Oneness?

When I could see and understand what a dancer truly meant to convey, it felt exciting and revelatory, like a flash of light.

At a 2019 Isha Foundation fundraiser for Cauvery Calling, a massive river revitalization effort, I watched a set of dances relating well-known tales of the woman named Cauvery, the wife of a renowned sage, who accepted the task of irrigating South India. At one point during the evening, the featured dancer told the story of another river, the Ganga, whose connection to India's history and mythology is as deeply rooted as Cauvery's. Though I'd heard many versions of Ganga's story, my skin prickled at this particular interpretation of the old tale:

Humanity needed Ganga's sacred waters on the Earth, and she was ordered to descend there from heaven. Angered by the order, Ganga planned to sweep the Earth away in a furious torrent. Appealed to for assistance, Shiva, the divine ascetic and yogi, caught Ganga as she descended in the thickly matted locks of his hair, where she remains now, eternally entangled. She is released only gradually, reliably, and sustainably for humanity's survival.

Locks. Entanglement. Sustainable release. In the context of the event and the information being shared there, I understood what the dancer wanted to tell me.

I saw that flash of light.

In the last few generations, forests flanking Indian rivers have been cleared for a variety of reasons, for example to follow non-traditional agricultural methods. For millennia, those forests produced thick, interlocking networks of roots and topsoil, which trapped water in the earth. That water was released gradually, feeding the river continuously and sustainably. The dense tree cover resulted in transpiration, drawing rainfall, and acting as another source of water for the river. The river never dried, and, due to the tightly-woven root networks, the monsoons couldn't wash away all of the nutrient-rich topsoil.

Encoded in the dance was this age-old wisdom. Shiva's locks represent the underground root-soil networks. Ganga's capture represents the sustainable release of water and preservation of topsoil. This is a story of the structures and cycles holding the water in our rivers. It's a story of the natural world in balance.

It is estimated that Indian land has supported agriculture for at least 10,000 years. However, over only the last few generations, the availability and nutritional value of its soil has plummeted due to climate change factors and the recent "Green Revolution" that encouraged farmers to abandon traditional crops, deploy chemical fertilizers, and plant high-yield seeds.

Lacking adequate water and nutrient-rich soil to produce crops, and now trapped in debt and despair, Indian farmers are committing suicide at a shocking rate—some sources estimate 60,000 suicides over the last three decades. This desperation has prompted responsive measures such as the Cauvery Calling campaign, an alliance of scientists, universities, associations, and government bodies.

Soil health is deeply connected to river health, and as such, soil depletion results in river depletion. Cauvery Calling is implementing a large-scale intervention, planting a kilometer-width of trees on both sides of the Cauvery, over her full length, in order to build up organic material in the soil, increase water percolation into the river, and promote water retention within the river. Farmers enrolled in the program are gradually diversifying to fruit tree-based agriculture and are receiving educational and moral support during the entire period of transition.

There is an old saying in the Tamil language: *even if the rains fail, Cauvery will never fail.* Sayings like these are now subject to question. Within a few generations, 10,000 years of traditional agriculture have come undone. Within a few generations, rivers that flowed for millennia have drained, and the forests that sustained nutrient-rich topsoil have been depleted.

It is now predicted that 25 percent of India will turn to desert. I find it unimaginable that this land I visited regularly, bursting with plants and insects, exploding with color and fragrance, overflowing with fruits and flowers, could lose its ability to support life—unimaginable that its teeming soil could turn to sand.

As this desertification advances, I wonder whether the erstwhile profession of water divination—the detection of drinkable water by examining local vegetation—might revive. The ancient sage Sarasvata composed a geo-botanical guide to prospect for groundwater based upon micro-environmental ecology, noting how, for example, the presence of a date palm near jujube and piu trees pointed to water, as did certain ficus varietals in proximity to one another. Later, in the 6th century C.E., Varahamihira built upon this work, listing 120 plants serving as groundwater indicators. Though such guides may possess less relevance due to irreparably damaged and altered landscapes, I suspect that the people drawn to this profession, being instinctively tuned to the natural world, will adapt.

I met such a figure recently, not in India, but in Santa Cruz, California. She was not a water diviner, but rather a forager who searched for edible foods among the grasses, weeds, and trees in the area.

When my husband and I began our hike with her, I found it difficult to concentrate, thinking of the wildfires that had raged in the area during the previous week, imagining another spark reigniting the landscape. But I slowly tuned in as the forager shared how to identify edible plants and explained which leaves and nuts and berries we could touch and eat. Each time, before placing an item in her mouth, she closed her eyes for a moment in gratitude to the land around her, the source of the food she consumed.

Though we hiked in a parched and dusty area, at one point we crossed into a clearing, its air fresh and cool. A pond rippled at our feet, inviting us to bend and touch the ground, to place our hands in the water.

I wished I could send myself backward in time to stop the car in India that held my child-self. I wished I could place her hands in the water, too. I'd ask her to feel Cauvery nourish the land, to look deeply into her waters.

I'd beg that child to ignore her various inconveniences. I'd ask her to stop worrying about pronunciations, to stop reciting city names, and instead to list all that the flowing water fed: *Soil* and *Clouds*, *Leaves* and *Roots*, *Bodies* and *Cells*.

Though I wouldn't want to spoil her moment of communion, I'd feel obligated to warn her of the times to come, and to urge her to fight for the water, for her life, for the earth.

Sources

1. Das, Krishna N. and Shyamantha Asoken. "A Quarter of India's Land Is Turning into Desert". ScientificAmerican.org. Nature Publishing Group. 18 June 2014. https://www.scientificamerican.com/article/a-quarter-of-india-s-land-is-turning-into-desert/
2. Isha Foundation. "Cauvery Calling". https://www.ishaoutreach.org/en/cauvery-calling
3. Kumar-Rao, Arati. "India's water crisis could be helped by better building, planning". NationalGeographic.com. National Geographic Society. 15 July 2019. https://www.nationalgeographic.com/environment/2019/07/india-water-crisis-drought-could-be-helped-better-building-planning/#close
4. Safi, Michael. "Suicides of nearly 60,000 Indian farmers linked to climate change, study claims". TheGuardian.com. Guardian Media Group. 31 July 2017. https://www.theguardian.com/environment/2017/jul/31/suicides-of-nearly-60000-indian-farmers-linked-to-climate-change-study-claims
5. Salopek, Paul. "India is in a historic water crisis. Will diverting 30 rivers solve it?" NationalGeographic.com. National Geographic Society. 6 March 2019. https://www.nationalgeographic.com/environment/2019/03/india-diverting-30-rivers-to-solve-historic-water-crisis/
6. Zwerdling, Daniel. "'Green Revolution' trapping its farmers in debt." Npr.org. Corporation for Public Broadcasting. 14 April 2009. https://www.npr.org/2009/04/14/102944731/green-revolution-trapping-indias-farmers-in-debt

Dheepa R. Maturi is a writer and poet who explores the relevance of ancient wisdom to modern life, particularly in the context of environmental health and sustainability. Her work has appeared in a variety of literary journals, including *Literary Hub, PANK, Entropy, Tweetspeak, Wanderlust*, and *Dear America: Reflections on Race*. Her prize-winning essay "We Are Trees" is forthcoming in an ecological anthology featuring the writing of Thich Nhat Hanh and a foreword by Pope Francis. She lives with her family in Indianapolis.

From the River to the Sea

The Reverend Emilie Teresa Smith

Marcia Mejia and her Indigenous community, the Eperara Nation, live along the banks of the Naya River in Colombia. Her settlement of Joaquincito sits right at the delta where the Naya reaches the Pacific Ocean. The Naya was a major site of conflict during the 50-year-long Colombian civil war. The Eperara, together with 64 Afro-descendant communities along the river, have defended their holy waterway and suffered terribly as narco-empires continue to fight for control of this strategic waterway.

1.

Marcia stamps her flip-flop on the dirty floor.

"I can't leave you, not with a whole two hours to go until the bus," she says in a low voice.

"Go, go," I say. "Go. I'll be fine. Be careful on the street."

We drop my bags on the sagging, tipping plastic seats in the terminal. We hug again. I brush back her straight black hair.

"You haven't had supper," she says.

"Nah."

I try not to cry. I'm old enough to be her mother, but I feel like her sister. She matters to me. I feel helpless, unable to do anything more to keep us close. She is so small, invisible to the rest of the world, so vulnerable. Steady, persistent, unstoppable, like a sturdy—but threatened—tree holding out her branches wide to protect her community: Joaquincito, of the Eperara Nation, on the mouth of the Naya River, on the Pacific Coast of Colombia.

The Eperara have lived on this river for time out of mind. But the enemies they face are monstrous, more dangerous perhaps than ever before: internal and foreign beasts crouching at the door. Waiting. Who will move in? Who has more power? Bigger guns? Who can twist things around, play the game—cocaine, mining companies, massive hydro-electric dams—make a pile, shit on the people and the earth, piss in the river, and move on?

"Go," I urge gently. "I've got food. Plantain chips and

lemonade made with panela. Besides, you guys have been feeding me too much for days. I already didn't fit into the canoa!" We both laugh.

"Okay, Emi," she says. She turns and walks away. Her orange wrap-skirt glows in the gloom. Somehow the bus station manages to be both fluorescent bright and deeply dingy at the same time. She's gone.

I take a deep breath. Alone at last. Time to think about where my heart has been and gone these past five days. I look around for my salt-crusted chips. Eat a few. I'm not that hungry. These have been days of fish, glorious starchy vegetables of different hues and sizes, and fruit I never knew existed.

Then, wait! The flash of orange is coming back! Marcia. Her face is crumpled.

"I *can't* leave you here alone. So long 'til the bus."

"It's good, really. Go. Go," I say.

"Okay, I'm leaving, Emi," says Marcia again, resigned. The orange in her beaded necklace, her orange skirt, her determined eyes set in her round face are all so dear to me. One final, final hug, and she's gone, becoming a carrot-colored dot, disappearing into the darkness. Just as she leaves, the evening rains call to the earth; the world outside is erased. Walls of water form, seeming to run both up and down.

I squeeze my eyes tight in prayer. Surround her with an impenetrable circle of protection. Make her invisible to the killers. Keep her safe. It's August, 2018. These are hard days for Colombian community leaders, especially for women and men from the Indigenous and Afro-descendant—Black—communities. More than 342 people have been killed in the past year-and-a-half, since the 2016 signing of the peace accords between the government and the guerrillas of the Rebel Armed Forces.

I had met Marcia three years earlier, at an international gathering in Brazil, Fe y Territorios, Faith and Territories. It was a busy, frantic conference, with hundreds of participants, but somehow Marcia connected with me. She sought me out time and again. We sat and chatted.

"You have to come see me someday, in my community," she said. I agreed, casually. I am the co-president of SICSAL, an international Christian human rights organization. Although we work in 28 countries, we are small and don't have a lot of funds. I had no idea when I would ever make it to Colombia.

Marcia and I weren't in touch regularly, but every once and a while, she would have access to the internet, and a note would pop up on my screen. Usually the same thing: How are you? When are you coming to see me?

Hi, I would answer. Nice to hear from you. Not sure.

But then, three years later, I *did* end up in Colombia, at another international conference, this time in Medellin. Marcia was supposed to come to the meeting but problems on the river took over: the boat couldn't get out. The level of violence on the river was very high. I had to admit, I didn't actually know *where* Marcia lived. Somewhere on a river delta, somewhere in Colombia. I didn't know how, exactly, to get to her.

Fortunately, I have friends.

La Comisión (the Interchurch Commission for Justice and Peace) makes the connections for me and sends me off on the night bus to Buenaventura. My companions are Nidiria, a poet, and her friend Yamali, young leaders from the Women's Committee of the Naya River Delta. They were both at the conference with me, showing up every day with one fabulous colorful outfit after another, purchased down in the city center during our breaks. At the conference they were clear: they had the right, as women, as young people, as the descendants of enslaved Africans, to live full lives, safely, in their homes, in their communities. Travelling with them, I feel like a young adventurer, invulnerable yet with a shake of danger.

The women shepherd me from the conference grounds, in the green sanctuary of the Mother Laura Convent on the outskirts of Medellin, through the long thin windy road down to the coast, through the sketchy, rough streets of Buenaventura to the safe house of the local Comisión leaders: Enrique and Maru—María Eugenia. The Comisión—on the frontline of energetic insistence on human rights for all—is a particular target for violence. The Inter-American Court of Human Rights has ordered the Colombian government to provide for the safety of Comisión leaders. We arrive at an anonymous-looking house. An armoured car is parked in front. An unsmiling guard stands stiffly; presumably he has a legal gun to protect us.

We arrive to a household waking up. Maru is making eggs, tossing her mop of curls as she stirs vigorously. She looks around to laugh hello and—snap—turns back to flip the arepas, fried cornmeal triangles. Enrique pours coffee. And, surprise! There are three human rights leaders here from the Washington Office on Latin America: Adam, Gimena and Alex. They are going upriver this very morning, all the way to Las Conchas. We can all go together, they say. I have no idea where Las Conchas is, but it's somewhere on Marcia's river, so—let's go!

The dock reeks. Things have died here and just been left to rot. An old wooden boat sits submerged up to its deck in water. Alongside it, men load two fiberglass hulls, which look sturdy enough. A group awaits, and then we're on board. The two boats sag full, about 10 or 12 people per vessel: four of us gringos, and the Comisión folks, my friends Nidiria and Yamali, going home. Most travellers are community members returning up the river, including baby Kaila and her mom, from Las Conchas. Kaila had been sick, and they brought her out to see a doctor. Now she sleeps right snug beside me, in her mother's arms, covered in a pink fuzzy sweater for the wind and the spray that will come. We slip on life jackets. Soon we putt-putt into the harbour. We slide past small shacks built up perilously over the river. Girls scrub clothes in the oily water, glancing up to see us just with the corner of an eye. We glide through the green and brown water and then into a mangrove swamp.

Now the boats move fast. They flit across the narrow waterways, choosing first the left branch, then the right from an impossible puzzle of choices. The boatsmen slip their caps over backwards and shout to each other with joy. It's like they're playing tag. The engine drones. The hum is so steady that I am almost asleep, head nodding down. Then—slap—we're in open ocean. Blue, white and grey. The silver curve of an ancient coin, across which are days and days of sea, until there are at last some distant, wistful islands. The sunlight is deceptively thin, but strong enough to burn Alex to a crisp in half an hour. I had remembered before we left and slipped on a light, long-sleeved shirt underneath my life jacket, despite the coastal heat.

Nudging, roaring, surging and soothing, the boatsmen know how to ride through the swells. Then at last we turn into the mangroves again. Nidiria calls loud and happy from the front, "Emi, THIS is the Naya!"

The Naya is a short river, only 120 kilometres long. It begins its life in the foothills of the soaring Andes and snake-winds its way down and across the jungle lowlands, becoming a fat and brown river at its mouth, thick with spindly mangroves, where it finally meets the Pacific Ocean. Indigenous peoples have lived along the rich banks of the Naya since before memory can tell. But life changed drastically when, in 1526, Spaniards arrived in the area.

That year, Sebastián de Belalcázar, a Castilian donkey thief, set out to pillage the hot lowlands of the Pacific littoral, founding the city of Cali, all the while slaughtering Indigenous people and fighting internecine battles with his fellow invaders. In the mountains beyond, rumours ran wild about rivers of gold and fabled cities paved with the shiny stuff. The Pizarro brothers had actually found stacks of treasure and went promptly to work destroying the great Inca Empire. Belalcázar, though, would find no such treasure.

Reported to be a particularly vicious man, Belalcázar was even called to account by the Spanish authorities for slaughtering all the women and children of a particular village while the men were absent. He died in 1555, while awaiting extradition to Spain, where he was to be tried for the murder of a fellow Spaniard. (The statue of Belalcázar in Cali was torn down in 2021 by Indigenous community members, as was one in Popayan a year earlier.)

There were no pots of gold to be had in the lowlands among the fishers and the gatherers, so Europeans set about creating sugar plantations. As the Indigenous communities were all but extinguished, the Spaniards began trafficking boatloads of Africans to slave in the fields. The slave trade began in 1518. Over the next three hundred-plus years an estimated 1.1 million Africans were forced through its hideous capital: Cartagena de Indias, on the Colombian Caribbean coast. Slavery was abolished in Colombia in 1852.

Today, along the Naya river, there are sixty-four Afro-Columbian communities, while the upriver and downriver Eperara peoples each have a reserve.

We buzz along the lower reaches of the river and, after about half an hour, pull up to a collection of wooden houses built on stilts. We land at a shaky ladder leading up to the Casa Grande, bigger by far than the small, personal homes. The Casa Grande is the sacred gathering space of Joaquincito, the home of the downriver Eperara people.

There she is! Marcia is waving madly and coming down the ladder. Everyone from the village is in the Casa Grande, waiting to meet me. Enrique and Maru are talking with Marcia, explaining that we're not staying, that I'm not staying, but that they'll drop me off the next day. "Do you want to come?" they ask her. "We're going to Las Conchas. You should come, but hurry, get your stuff."

Marcia disappears, then returns with a little pink backpack and a girl, maybe about nine years old. They jump in the back. We beam with joy at one another. We did it! We're together at last. There is no time to say anything, and we're off. Up the river, buzz, buzz.

The green walls of the jungle close in around us, hiding who knows what. The trees seem endless, eternal. Looks like the jungle won here. But then we zip around a corner and there's a big town: Puerto Merizalde, named after its founding bishop, who dreamed of building a bustling metropolis in the jungle. We move along the wooden houses stacked right over the river until—there He is! Standing high on top of a massive cathedral in the river town that had failed to become a city, right on the dome reaching out to his people: a grandiose white Jesus, hands extended in blessing. We float along under his outstretched arms.

On the other side of town, we dock and climb out onto a soggy wooden platform. We're stopping for lunch. At last Marcia and I hug each other. I meet Yasmin, her daughter. We head up arm in arm to a table to my first fish of the Rio Naya. We eat with satisfaction, and we catch up. Things are not well at all on the river. Peace accords have meant nothing. I listen, shake my head. Four community leaders dead in the last few months. Everything a great unknown. Solemnly we board the boats again to travel to the next stop upstream. Yamali stays here, but Nadiria will travel with us up to Las Conchas.

2.

We're heading further inland. After about an hour, we arrive at the Humanitarian Zone of San Francisco, where we will exchange our ocean-going boat for a river boat that will make it easier to journey farther up the shallow river through the ever-thickening, verdant jungle.

The region around the Naya River has a particularly troubled history, explains Enrique from the Comisión, with input from the WOLA experts, Adam and Gimena. In the past thirty years or so the Naya's relatively short length, from the thick coca leaf sites up in the highlands, along the back and forth of the main branches of the river, to the lonely and unguarded Pacific coast, has become a key route for the moving of drugs and arms. There are big bucks to be made by the Colombian military (the largest in Latin America) and the shady paramilitary bands (which have direct links to the official military, but operate with impunity). These latter are responsible for the greatest number of human rights abuses. Last of all, but thick in the game, are Colombia's two guerrilla organizations: the Rebel Armed Forces (FARC) and the much smaller yet still fierce National Liberation Army (ELN). Everyone wants a piece of this rich pie.

During Holy Week, 2001, one of the worst massacres of Colombia's more than 50-year-long civil war occurred along the Naya River. Between April 11th and 12th, paramilitaries from the United Self-Defense Forces of Colombia brutally murdered and mutilated an estimated 70 people up and down the Naya. Thousands more fled into hiding along tributary rivers, to Puerto Merizalde, and all the way down the river and along the ocean into the city of Buenaventura.

After a number of years of displacement, communities started to return and rebuild. An important tool for peacemaking was granted to them when the Inter-American Court on Human Rights ordered precautionary measures for the communities, and a number of "humanitarian zones" were declared. These were to be areas exclusively for civilians, entirely free from all weapons. No armed players from any side of the war would be allowed into the Zones. The communities would patrol themselves, and the Naya Community Council would oversee the civilian network.

By the time we arrive at the San Francisco Humanitarian Zone, I'm feeling a bit queasy. Maybe it's the food, the sun, or the sway of the boat. I breathe deeply. We all pile out. Good thing Maru told us to wear our flip-flops. We disembark straight into the shallow water, and the riverbed is muddy and rocky. We are met by community leaders at the river's edge. The village reaches right down to the water. Old cement block buildings, once painted but now crumbly and worn, stand close together. Neighbors look out and shout out to us. We stop at one place and another. Everyone knows Enrique and Maru, and there's laughing and teasing. At one place we are given a shot glass to share. I take a wee sip. Holy Beasts! There is a coal of fire in my mouth, in my throat, in my esophagus, in my gut. Oh, I remember this. Isabelino, an Afro-Colombian leader who I met in Brazil, had some. It is a sacred drink, made with herbs, but also with a high alcohol content. My stomachache eases. That's good news!

Then, out of nowhere, a helicopter thunders overhead. It lands on the other side of the village. The army. We go closer to observe. Soldier after soldier, each shouldering a bundle, marches down from behind a hill, turns left and disappears. We watch them warily from a distance, then go down to the next street. The leaders tell us what is going on. The soldiers have set up camp, smack at the edge of the village, on a jutting bit of land sticking into the curve of the river.

Adam, who carries himself with calm and confidence, consults with the villagers. Leaving them behind, we gringos move forward to check in with the military camp. An infantry specialist comes out to see us, a little surprised. Adam and Gimena converse with him, and Alex and I fall back. Soldiers should not be here, while we have every right. We are invited guests and, of course, we are unarmed. Quietly I take out my phone and snap a few shots. The soldiers have brought in heaps of provisions, what look like sacks of sugar or rice. Everyone is polite if tense.

I get the story in pieces. Officially, it seems, the military came to search for evidence concerning the four community leaders—three brothers and a cousin—who were kidnapped, disappeared and in the end murdered in April and May. Adam raises his eyebrows.

Later, I get a few more pieces of the puzzle. Valle de Cauca, a distant, forgotten corner of Colombia, became a central battle-ground and hiding place for the fighters in the civil war. It was mostly controlled by FARC guerrillas. After the 2016 peace accords went into effect, the FARC disbanded, moving into controlled de-escalation communities. But along the Naya, this left a vacuum of power, and of course the movement of drugs continues. There is a lot of money involved. Adam says that he has heard that ordinary soldiers request to be sent to this region. This is the place to make money. That may be the real reason the army is here. And behind the army, the paramilitary waits.

Finally, we are back at the boat, a new one able to go further up the river. I climb in beside Marcia's daughter, Yasmin, in the front row, the bumpiest place. The green jungle walls climb higher and higher on either side of us, as the river gets both shallower and narrower. A couple of lime-green iguanas scuttle into the brush. There's no more sun to burn us—it's rumbling and cloudy up in the darkening heavens. Occasional single wooden houses jut up on stilts, and every once in a while, another Humanitarian Zone, with its big vinyl sign declaring it to be a weapons-free area, exclusively for civilian use. There are children running along the shore, people in impossibly skinny dugout canoes, standing or sitting, and others leaning on the window frames of the houses. Everyone waves, on the water and on the land.

The boat sways and swoops. On one riverbend intersection we come across, incredibly, my friend Isabelino, who had given me a sip of the sacred drink when we were in Brazil. We wave and laugh, and then our boats charge off like horses to gallop in opposite directions. The boat drones. I'm not sure we'll ever get there. We haven't seen houses for a while, when on one swoop we hear a sickening scrape and thud. Then the engine dies. Our boat turns lazily in the current and starts floating aimlessly downstream. Where will we stop? Sometimes it's better not to ask anything and just encomendarse (hand yourself over) to God.

Our able boatman manages to get us into one quiet lull on the river's edge and then another. Going backwards, we come to a house high on the riverbank. He calls up. A gruff answer comes down. Then a man appears with a rifle of some sort. Shouting, suspicion back and forth. It looks like he won't help. Are we going to have to float down further? But then, it seems, peace has been made. The man on the shore disappears, comes back and down to our boat. He has a thin white wire. The motor is raised out of the water. I hold my breath and look around. Everyone seems relaxed. Then we all cheer as the engine putt putts. We're off again.

The going is tenuous, with the driver occasionally killing the motor. We are too heavy, and the river too shallow. Once or twice, we get out of the boat and walk along a sandbar. At one point, Alex, who's a big man, falls into the river while exiting the boat. But there's not one complaint, just a smiling resignation at riding the rest of the way in his wet jeans.

Rain rushes down. Tarps appear from the boat's storage, and we wrap them around ourselves. I tuck the end in around Yasmin. She's shivering. I take off my sunscreen shirt and wrap it around her, and then the tarp, and then my arm holding it all in place. Then it happens: I love her. This little girl, who has the bravest mother: Marcia, who has traveled to Spain and to the States, who has seen and touched and laughed at snow, who has macheted her way through every rock planted on her path, a rural Colombian Indigenous woman with no recognized rights. Her sheer will is making things happen.

At every bend in the river Enrique drapes himself off the bow of the boat, holding tight to an oar, and measures for depth. For a long time, it is announced that Las Conchas is 15 minutes away, just around the next corner, until, at last, half of us are dumped onto a sandbar while the boat makes its final push to the community. Then comes back for the others. It is dark, and the rain is torrential. We were supposed to arrive at noon, and now it's seven in the evening. In all the boat trip took almost nine hours.

We shake our feathers out in a dry little house on stilts. Baby Kaila, who didn't cry once during the trip, and her mother are welcomed joyously, and Kaila disappears into the arms of one auntie and then another, and then through a series of cousins, or sisters and brothers. Her mother rests after the long ride. Nidiria sits and laughs with her old friends. The WOLA people talk softly with our hosts.

At last we make our way in the dark, in the rain, up a walkway that has become a stream, to a school. We sit at the small desks, and the room fills up. Someone jerry-rigs a lightbulb and a microphone to a cord which goes out the window to a generator somewhere. More neighbours come. The room is packed. People stand thick along the outside of the barred windows.

Before we talk, a smaller group of men and women gather in front of the classroom, to drum, to sing. How could I ever describe this sound, not even music, exactly? How could I, with my thin-white-Nordic blood, ever say anything at all about what this drumming and singing means? Something so ancient, so holy, so filled with sorrow and resistance, struggle and survival of 15-20 generations from the capture of their ancestors in Africa. If this isn't Resurrection, I don't know what is. The shaking, the lament, the song of determination fills the room, fills the hearts and souls of everyone present, pressing us all into a bonded commitment, a kind of vow that can never be broken. When they finish at long last, I don't know what else needs to be said. The woman leading the singing says one thing: "This is a song of gratitude, and welcome. Thank you." I lower my head. My eyes burn.

But of course, there *is* more to be said. One person after another speaks a part of the story. Adam types away on his computer, which came upriver sealed in a freezer-size Ziploc bag.

On April 17th, three men, brothers Hermes Angulo Zamora and Obdulio Angulo Zamora and their cousin, Simeón Olave Angulo, disappeared from somewhere along the river. After they failed to return, community members searched up and down the waterways. They reported the disappearance to government officials in Buenaventura. Tensions continued to climb. A third brother, Iber Angulo Zamora, was increasingly threatened. Support was again demanded from the departmental capital.

At last, on May 5th, a commission from the Human Rights Ombudsman office came to escort Iber out of the region. On the water they were confronted by armed men in a boat, who pulled Iber into their possession and sped away. Later, the four disappeared men were found executed.

Fears are high that the army is using these murders as an excuse to move in and take over the region. And right behind them, the paramilitaries. The river is, some community leaders say, already surrounded by the army, who have no regard for the communities' ways of practicing vigilance. Nidiria points out that for more than 300 years Afro-descendant communities have defended and conserved the river and the earth. There is hope for increased unity between Afro and Indigenous people of the Naya.

There is some debate around small-time coca farmers, up and down the river. These farmers have never become wealthy but have served as a source for the raw coca leaves. Coca farmers are trapped. They have few other options. The government promised to help with new crops, and thousands of farmers signed contracts stating that they will no longer plant coca. But as usual, those getting shafted are the already poor. There has been no meaningful support for the transition, and in the meantime, the power struggle to control the coca trade ratchets up, with farmers trapped in the middle.

The discussion carries on for hours. Lollipops and chocolate cookies are distributed at some point. Finally the gathering comes to an end. I sit up quickly when Enrique asks if I might pray with the community.

"Of course," I say. How to pray here in this place, with these people, what can I possibly say? Thank God for the Holy Spirit who always gives the words to speak. I think, well, why not start the prayer like I start every prayer. Not sure if it will work here.

"El Señor sea con ustedes," I say.

"Y con tu espíritu," comes thundering back, more people than I can count.

And so, in the dim flickering light, in the pouring rain, in a schoolhouse in Las Conchas I close my eyes and we pray.

3.

It rains all night in Las Conchas. There's not a sound in the little dry house, except for a dog—there's always a dog. Bark. Bark. Bark. But I sleep completely senseless, wiped out from so much travelling, listening, until the first roosters crack the morning chorus.

We are up with the first light. We eat soda crackers and drink hot, sweet coffee. Then we go back down the river, so much faster than the day before. The shallow areas from yesterday have filled in with last night's rain. It's still blustery and even cold, especially in the fast boat. Marcia and I make a Yasmin sandwich, and we wrap ourselves all up in tarps. There are children in school uniforms in the thin canoas, standing up and pushing along the river's edge. Today's the first day of school, after holidays, and they are heading to the nearest classroom. Yasmin whispers to me, "We have school today too." I have no idea how far we still have to go downriver. Go, boat, go!

We arrive in San Francisco. No sign of the soldiers. We change boats and float down past the giant Jesus frozen in eternal blessing.

Before long we spy Joaquincito. It's still morning, about 9 o'clock. Marcia, Yasmin and I disembark, climb the wooden stairs. The WOLA folks and the Comisión people wave and push off. About a month, Adam yells over the motor, until they'll have their official WOLA report on the Naya River. We duck under the low roof and step in—suddenly we're in the Casa Grande. It is dark, cool. I imagine it full of people for ceremonies and meetings.

So, here I am. Now what? Surrender, open, trust, love. Plutarco comes out to greet us. He's the head of the community. Later I find out he's Marcia's older brother and the community health promoter.

Joaquincito is the Resguardo, the reserve of the Eperara community of the lower Naya River. There are about a hundred Indigenous nations all over Colombia, settled from the lowland rivers that head west to the Pacific, or north to the Caribbean, or east to join the great Amazon, to the highlands that meet the mountains and the edge of the Andes. In Joaquincito there are 42 households, mostly Indigenous, with just a few Afro or Mestizo families blended in. Along the river there are far more Afro-descendant settlements,

30 times as many as Indigenous communities.

Marcia leads me to the other side of the Casa Grande, through a wooden kitchen with a fire pit rigged up on cement blocks with a sand base. There's the biggest cooking pot I've ever seen—upside down now. That must feed everybody.

"We just had a big feast," says Marcia. "Five days ago."

We shimmy down a treacherously (for me) damp wooden ladder, across some soft planks, then up onto a long, cement platform, about three feet above the wet ground.

"That's the bridge," says Marcia. "We fought years for that. Blood was spilt for it." The bridge stretches out along the front of the houses. Each house reaches the bridge with a simple plank. Drainage canals carve into the land, which is often underwater depending on the level of the river, which floods with heavy rain and the sway of the ocean's tide.

We go down two, three, four houses to Plutarco's place.

"We'll stay next door, with my mother," says Marcia. "But it's more comfortable here." We slip inside. "I'll get breakfast."

I meet Plutarco's wife, Paula. There are piles of kids, Plutarco and Paula's children, Paula Andrea, Paulo Andres, Junior and little Ingrid. And Marcia's son, Alejandro. Then comes Marcia's mother up the plank, carrying two full, sloshing pails of water from the river. She nods a greeting to me and snaps a few words in Siapidara.

I sit in a chair at a small table. Marcia has disappeared through a door and left me with the kids. They are taking turns swinging in a hammock. Ingrid, who is one and a bit, stares at me with a look of suspicion as she moves from sister's hip to cousin's arms, then back again. Who's this woman, say her fierce undisguised eyes.

Marcia comes back in a bit with a plate piled with food—just for me. Yikes. Four boiled green bananas, a hill of rice and a piece of rich pink pork. "That's from the feast," she says. "My brother smoked it. It takes a long time, but it lasts then for a good while, about a week." Of course. There's no refrigeration here, only electricity once in a while with an expensive generator.

Dear Lord, I'm in Rio Naya bacon heaven! Who knew that pork could be this delicious? Greasy and meaty and smoky. The green bananas are starchy and bland, perfect with a piece of bacon embedded.

While I'm finishing up a great fuss is going on in the house across from me—later I find out it's the general store, which enjoys the only constant electricity, provided by a large solar panel. We head out to see. José de la Cruz has hunted an animal in the night, and now it's coming to be weighed, and sold, I presume. I ask what it is, and get "rabbit" and "wild pig" as answers. The beast is now headless, so I can't really tell. Not by looking at its little trotters. A sharp thin knife carves it into pieces.

After this, Marcia calls me to go back to the Casa Grande. There's going to be a community meeting—a chance for me to get to know more people. We gather in the cool dark space. We sit on wide platform benches, men, many women, and many more children. Plutarco greets me officially. I say thank you, and then I listen.

Arturo, the school teacher, speaks first: "We are one of 102 different nations in what is now called Colombia. After the Spanish invasion we were called savages, then we were called, pejoratively, "minors" or infants. In 1991 there were reforms to the national law and we were recognized as nations, and the Afro-descendant communities were as well. We lived in peace. Then in 2001 we suffered the terrible internal displacement. We fled to Buenaventura, to other rivers, and no one helped us. We returned, and we know our rights, but so far that is just on paper. In 1989 the limits of our Reserve were defined, then in 2005 they were extended. There has been some disagreement with the Afro-community, but there has been a lot of work on building unity. The government owes us a lot, and we have received barely anything. Now, for example, they are saying something ridiculous: We own the land, as Indigenous people, but the government owns what's under the land. That makes no sense to us."

Oh dear, I think. The mining companies are already hovering here. Possibly Canadian. Beware.

Then Inez speaks: "I am the head of the Women's Association. We have had a lot of troubles. The government promised us support, but nothing at all has arrived. Then there were the fumigations. We lost everything: even our seeds. We had yams and yucca, sugarcane and plantains. We lost most of it. The earth no longer yields much. We've had to go further and further into the forest, away from the village."

Norberta speaks: "We don't want mining or any such thing. We haven't asked for much, but we haven't received anything at all.

We need a health centre, a school, decent housing. We've had no support since the displacement in 2001. We have insisted that there be dialogue. We are tired after 52 years of war. Our young people don't want war. We live in paradise here. We have taken care of this place, we have looked after our own. They don't want to admit that the military are here, and the paramilitaries, but we know that they are around. This is a Reserve, not a Humanitarian Zone like they have up the river. But this is a weapons-free zone too. Twice the army has arrived in the community, and twice the community has chased them off. All the Naya River has been in resistance. We have been fighting for 527 years, with our own culture, language and art. The last straw was the fumigations in 2012 and 2013."

Cecilia agrees: "Everything was lost. The earth herself got sick. Our food supplies have diminished. Our pineapple, for example. And we live in fear. We built our Sacred Big House in 1991, and we have been saying forever: Mother Earth is not to be destroyed, not our forests. This is the very heart, soul, strength of the Earth. We are the only Indigenous community on the lower Naya, and we have been fighting militarization and big companies. And now they are threatening to fumigate again."

The meeting goes on until many have spoken. I feel like I'm starting to get a sense of the story. Just a taste.

Marcia invites me to go back to the house. They are going to carry on in meeting. I am exhausted. I need a nap. I think fondly of the hammock as I negotiate my way up the slippery plank to Plutarco's house. But what do I find? Ingrid is sleeping in the hammock, across its soft width, a perfect little bundle. I am embarrassed at how grouchy I feel: here I am uncomfortable and tired—and jealous of a baby!

Marcia is away in the Casa Grande for a long time. I'm glad she doesn't feel like she has to entertain me constantly. I sit and read my book by the Andean theologian Victor Bascopé, the man who showed me how to make coca leaf tea and how to chew coca leaves when I was in Ecuador. He had told me about how hard it was to research the detailed story of the invasion of the Spaniards. The murder of so many leaders, both named and those now forgotten, and so many others. The treasures that were stolen, and much, much worse, the theft, destruction, attempted annihilation of Andean cosmology.

"When I look at the rocks making up the walls and churches and colonial buildings I just cry," says Victor. "Each stone is an ancestor."

I am reading about the nosebleed-high Andes, and I am here in the warm always-wet lowlands. The people and stories are linked, though not the same, of course. The invasion narratives of the Spanish, the Portuguese, the English and the French have common threads. For King, for Queen, for Church.

At last, Marcia's back from the meeting. They aren't going to Buenaventura tomorrow after all. Not until Wednesday. I can go with them. Marcia's worried that I haven't had lunch. I'm stuffed, I reassure her. She's trying so hard to help me, to guess what I need. I am still figuring out how to be here. Mostly I try not to be a nuisance. Whatever may be uncomfortable or different or not the way I would do it. Forget it! Receive everything. I am filled with gratitude.

We go to the sacred river. Yasmin comes, and little Paula joins us. Everyone jumps into the river. Even though we're in the warm equatorial waters, I have to ease myself in, down the worn ladder. The water is brown and slow and cool. Once I'm in, the river seems wide and endless. We splash and play. Marcia washes herself, and then a tub of clothes, while sitting on a low wooden step. The girls pretend to be sharks, and they do cartwheels from the soft bank into the water. They are like baby otters, twisting and splashing and smiling. They find a canoa, and they paddle around and around. They convince me to get in, and around we go, laughing without walls of any kind.

This river is holy. It is the artery of the whole body, the means by which people here live. It is where they bathe and wash and pull water for everyday things. It is their means of travel and their source of fish. The river changes, with the tides and the cycles of the moon and the rains.

"Naya Tooja." Sacred River Naya, Marcia whispers. "Cho nara weda tooja beda." No human hand could have ever made this river. No human hands dug the channels or made the turns. We float, and more than that: we are carried.

4.

It rains all night again, and I sleep in Marcia's bed—without Marcia—with the mosquito netting all tucked in around in the absolute dark, in the absolute silence, but for the roosters that set one another off, then call down the row at three, four, five in the morning. By five or six o'clock, I know, everyone will be getting up. There was one single shattering of thunder last night—I didn't see the schism of lightning. It was after we were in bed around nine and it seemed to crack the wooden houses with the power of its sound. Yasmin began to cry. Her mother's soft words pulled her back into sleep, to comfort, to shelter.

Again, I wonder what I can do, what I can say? It takes so much energy to host me, to welcome me, to worry about me, to make space for me. Would it be better if I did something in a different way? Why am I here? Of course, I am not the Great White Saviour. But is there some part of me that wants to be? I have nothing to offer but my self. Marcia is clear, and she has shared with others: Emilie doesn't come to bring projects or money.

Yet there is something about me being here—for me, and for the community. What does it mean that someone sees, someone notices, someone listens? For them and for me. I lie and think and toss a little. The rain comes down in steady soft waves along the roof. In a while, it is not quite as dark as it used to be.

At last it is five or so, and we get up. The day starts. Children are sleepy, still staying close to home, and to mothers. The women go into the wet side of the house. I am starting to figure it out. The front of the house is the 'dry' part. Here people sleep, sometimes in a separate room walled off, and in the back is where the cooking and washing happens, in a room still up on stilts. The back food-area is divided too, the preparing side and the washing part—where dishes and fish, root vegetables and even babies are rinsed and scrubbed—and then out on the very edge a fire on a bed of sand and stone. The back area opens to the sides and the bright green everywhere of growing things. This room is where the action is, at least in the daytime. Grandmas and mothers and aunties and kids gather here. Another hammock and a few small stools are occupied, so I sit on the floor. I like it better here than on my own on the other side of the wooden wall, where I spent the afternoon reading yesterday. Plutarco comes in with a mess of fish, and Marcia's peeling green bananas. For now, we drink sweet hot coffee and eat soda crackers while the fish get cleaned.

I'm starting to understand food here now too. All meals seem to be a starch and a protein. Starches so far have been yucca, taro, purple yams, and green banana. The first three, and the last too sometimes, are prepared boiled. Twice we have the bananas fried, once whole, and once squashed into disks, patacones. The proteins we eat are best bacon ever, eggs, lots of fish, boiled or fried, beans, and once, chicken—but we'll get to that part later. Everything is so good. Then there's the fruit: sugarcane (peeled, sucked and chewed, spitting the hard, twiggy part out), green coconuts (drinking the fresh water first, then eating the thin, slippery bits inside after cracking open with a machete), guanabana, grenadilla, cherimoya, pitaya (weird yellow blobby thing with black spots, mushy white and melting inside), lulo (only for juice), papaya, maracuya (passion fruit? eat together with crunchy seeds), bacao which I thought was cacao, and is indeed a relative (very strong smell and taste, bitter crossed with sour, inedible for me—I give it to happy, receiving children), bananas and plantains, which I only see cooked and green, and my favourite: zapote—pumpkin orange, sweet and slimy, with two fat, long, slippery brown seeds. The zapote is given to me as I walk along the raised cement platform by a young man rushing by with two of them. He stops and turns when he sees me, and hands me one of his treasures.

The fruit is all gift. People come by the house to deliver or call me into their house across the wooden plank. I receive everything, try everything, like everything (except the bacao).

Doña Cecilia particularly likes to come by. She talks to me, and she asks me questions. She invites me to her house. "My house is really clean," she says, and she shows me around the yard, back a bit from the cement platform and along another platform, this one made of wood. Her yard is a little bit drier—at least for now—as it is farther from the slow, mud-brown river that rises up every twenty days or so and floods under the closer houses. She shows me where she has a raised compost pile. She shows me her flowers, her fruit trees and her medicinal herbs—she and her husband, Bejerano, are healers. "This one is for stomach upset, this for headache, this for (mal de) ojo, this for sadness." She takes me—and a whole handful of children—up a narrow path that leads even farther away from the river. We should have gumboots, she says, eyeing my flip-flops skeptically. We wander up the squashy path until it is apparent that it just won't work. The earth is too soft. I am ankle deep in mud. Further up, she points, we have our plantings, the yams, and papas chinas (taro). She tells me more about how terrible it has been since the fumigations.

The Colombian government, with the full support of the USA and its 'war on drugs,' has engaged in extensive spraying for years. The chemical defoliant, glyphosate—the main toxic component in Monsanto's Roundup—was repeatedly sprayed in aerial raids on coca plants and—according to residents of the Naya River basin—everything else: food crops, houses, animals and even people. In 2015 the government promised to stop fumigations by airplane after the World Health Organization declared that glyphosate was a proven carcinogen. However, the threat of resumed spraying remains, the latest possibility being drones to deliver the poison.

"So many things have just dried up," says Doña Cecilia, sadly. "No pineapple at all. Nothing is growing in some areas." People have told me of strange diseases not known in these regions before. Marcia's mother had to endure the choppy boat ride to Buenaventura and have a large tumour removed from her neck.

Don Bejerano shows me his carvings: a sweet little turtle, a bird, and a gorgeous walking stick carved with a couple of birds, and just below the handle, a man, holding a staff of his own and a mochila, a woven bag.

Doña Cecilia worries at the fire and brings me my first fried fish of the day—crispy with salt sizzled right through. I pick at it and eat it delicately, saving on the side bones thinner than a needle. Her grandson comes by, and Doña Cecilia sends him up a palm tree to get us a couple of fresh coconuts. He sheds his shoes and shimmies up fast, but stops about two-thirds of the way up. He yells something down to his grandma, then scoots down quickly.

"There's a new wasp's nest up there!" they explain to me, laughing. We'll have to wait for our drinks.

As we share stories—I tell them about my red-headed grandson and my black shaggy dog—I can feel the threads begin to connect us. Doña Cecilia tells me about her son, who died, about how heartbreaking and constant is her desolation. Once, she says, a long time ago, she tried to live somewhere else; her husband is from the Chocó region, but she could never get used to not being on the Naya. She tells me her story of the displacement in 2001.

It was further up the river, in the Afro communities where the worst violence took place. By various estimates, between 40 and 130 civilians were killed over a few days, many brutally. Bodies were dissected with a chainsaw. Quickly, the information flew down the river: leave, now, get out. Most everyone did. It was a massive exodus of boats, big and small. Some went into the town of Puerto Merizalde to stay with family, many went into hiding along quieter branches of the river. And others went all the way to Buenaventura. The whole river was drained of people. Doña Cecilia says that at first they refused to go. But at last Doña Cecilia, Don Bejerano, and their children climbed onto a boat. They made it downriver, to a branch along the mangroves where they hid for five days.

Then they decided to go back, no matter what. Five families returned to Joaquincito together. They stayed in one house, afraid of the paramilitaries, who were hunting up and down the river. They stayed and ate what they could.

"The worst thing was listening to the dogs and the chickens die. We had nothing to feed them, and almost everyone had gone. They didn't have time to take their animals. The animals cried and cried from the pangs of hunger, and finally they died. The Sisters (from the order of Mother Laura) heard we were starving and brought us a little bit of food, dried rice and beans. We held out for a few weeks, but in the end, we had to travel down to the city, to Buenaventura, where for two years we lived as refugees."

We sit quietly together. I am thinking about the recent murders on the river, the ongoing deaths, the attacks on leaders of all social organizations. Back at the conference in Medellin, we named and prayed for the over three hundred Colombian community leaders murdered since the signing of the Peace Accords, two years ago.

We sit and then I go back with the flock of children to Plutarco's house. We eat more fried fish, soft and salty, which never seems to be too filling. Marcia's sister-in-law drops by, with a young woman—her daughter-in-law—and her brand-new baby grandson. We chat, and I hold the baby, and then, when it seems polite, hand him back to his mother. The women consult for a while in Siapidara. I smile nicely. Marcia comes up to me and asks me quietly, "They want you to baptize the baby."

My heart thuds. What to do? How can I be both pastoral and stay within the bounds of acceptable church practice? I know I can do the former and don't always trust myself with the latter.

The only important question in this instant is: What would be of assistance to this family? What do they need? I don't worry about correctness within the church, but *do* I care about being honest with this family. Baptism is a mark of belonging. Of course, all creation, and every creature, especially this perfect little one with dark hair and black eyes, lying in my arms, is loved, adored, treasured by his family—and by the One who made us all. Baptism is a way we humans turn and shout yes back to God.

There is no priest or pastor who ever visits this community. And me? I am, now, a friend. I say yes, let's bless the baby! Let's get some water. They bring me clean water, from the big jugs of filtered water left for me by the prepared WOLA people. We pour a bowlful. We gather around, the children and the women. I hold little Liam Mejia. We pray together. May the Creator of Heaven and Earth ever hold you close, little one. May you flourish in love, in this place. May you grow to the fullness of your life. May you play in this river for many, many years. May the fruit be abundant. May the pineapples return.

In my heart I pray that the wolves of greed and violence that surround this community may be held at bay. I pray that the Naya won't be invisible to the world. That the Afro communities standing for their right to live, to flourish, may be allowed to exist as signs of the bursting through of justice. And that the Indigenous communities may be left to practice their knowledge, their time-out-of-mind knowing of things that matter. So many things that we have forgotten. And I pray that we—the rich, the north—can turn our hearts away from greed and towards love for all creation.

Liam is asleep. He moves and stretches a little as the water pours off of his head, onto the wooden floor, through the cracks, and back to the water below.

Earlier in the day, as I peered out of the wooden morning window and out along the cement walkway, I saw a woman carrying two unfortunate upside-down chickens. They seemed to have given up, no squawking was happening as their tails pointed to the sky. Uh no, I thought. Too much. Has Marcia asked for them to be brought to me here? I *am* being a nuisance. I nodded as the woman approached, then sighed in relief as she walked by our plank, down one, two, three doors, and up to another house.

But now, after our blessing, I'm told that there is a chicken soup coming back to Plutarco's house. The chickens were killed to celebrate this impromptu baptism. I am served a big bowl. Liam sleeps and we eat.

Later I spy his mother with a whole group of young women and men out on a raised platform playing soccer with a squashed, wet ball. Every few minutes the ball flies off into the mud and the water on the ground. Then it starts raining. No one stops playing, laughing, shouting, and the game goes on until the sun hovers over the western bank of the river.

Just before it sinks into the jungle trees, Marcia and I go along the cement platform, then along the wooden walkway to the holy river, to her most holy river, her cho nara weda tooja beda, her ancestral river, made by no human hands. Here we sit and dangle our feet into the warm water. Tomorrow, before dawn, we will be going out to the open sea, through waves rolling bigger than our boat, to Buenaventura—one of the most dangerous cities in Colombia—she with Plutarco to settle things, to fight with the state, me to catch a bus back to the Convent of Mother Laura in Medellin, and a plane back to Canada. We feel sad already. I will go with my heart made bigger, my life somehow different. Marcia—who knows why she reached out to me, what she saw, what she sees?

It doesn't matter. This is how two women become friends.

Afterword

This essay was written in 2019-2021. Since my visit I have had steady, if laconic, exchanges with Marcia. Sea changes have happened in her life, and in Colombia. In January 2020 Marcia welcomed a new baby, with her husband, Colombian Indigenous activist, Wilson Poirama. In June 2022, Marcia began advanced studies at the Pontifical University in Medellin.

Marcia writes, "Agradecer primero a mi dios por darme una

oportunidad de vivir y también a mis amigo internacinale que me ayudaron para mí salud y esa es la razón de vivir en este planeta tierra, agradecer a mi esposo wilson poirama por apoyar mis metas, mis carrera profesional, en todas mis proyecion, tambien familiares como hermano, hermanas, mi madre querida, mis hijos gracias a todos asi puedo avanzar nueva mente encontrar en la universidad"

Translation: "First of all, I would like to thank my god for giving me an opportunity to live and also my international friends who helped me with my health (crisis), and that is the reason for living on this planet Earth; I would like to thank my husband Wilson Poirama for supporting my goals, my professional career, in all my plans, also relatives like my brother, sisters, my dear mother, my children; thanks to all so I can advance again in the university."

There are hopeful changes at the national level as well. In August 2022, Gustavo Petro, a former guerrilla and the ex-mayor of Bogotá and, thrillingly, Francia Márquez were inaugurated as President and Vice-President of Colombia. Márquez, an Afro-descendant woman from Cauca, a renowned and\ beloved community leader and anti-mining activist, has invited her countrypeople to join her in living a "vida sabrosa", a life with flavor, a life with dignity, joy and power. Popular movements are gathering strength.

Adam and Gimena from the Washington Office on Latin America have kept their eyes on the Colombian story, especially watching and reporting on the risks and triumphs of local community leaders. Here is their fine article summarizing the current context.[1]

I plan to visit Marcia in March 2023, as part of the gathering of the Óscar Romero International Christian Network in Solidarity with the Peoples of Latin America (SICSAL).

1. https://www.wola.org/analysis/five-priorities-for-a-new-era-of-u-s-colombia-relations/

Emilie Teresa Smith is an Argentine-born Canadian Anglican priest, writer and theologian. Since 1984 she has walked with a profound commitment to the people of Guatemala. In 2012 she was elected co-president of the historic Oscar Romero International Liberation Theology Network (SICSAL). Since then she has visited every region of Latin America and the Caribbean, and has been privileged to come alongside numerous community struggles for the protection of sacred land and water.

Swimming Whole

E. C. Barrett

First Jeff Martin bought the narrow strip of land between the river and Banks Road from the town, then he spider-webbed caution tape between the trees and nailed posted signs to their bark. The swimming hole where so many of us had spent our childhood summers was no longer ours. And this with each year hotter than the last.

Martin, who also owned *The Weekly Gazette*, the Dollar Store on the edge of town, and a quarter of the rental properties, bought and moved into the Carter Mansion across the street from our swimming hole after the last owner died. As big as it was, it wouldn't pass as a mansion nowadays, but the historical plaque in front of it named it the original home of the town founder. A draw, no doubt, for Martin, who fancied himself a self-made man in the way the wealthy who grew up just shy of wealthy tend to do. He didn't live there one full summer before he convinced the town council that the strip of land—the only spot with passable access down the river-cut gorge—was nothing more than a waste of taxpayer money.

Why pay to have it mown, when he could send his landscape crew over? (And seeing as he was doing the town this favor, really, the property ought to be tax-exempt, didn't they agree?) Like most things Jeff Martin said and did, it had the sound of a gift bestowed. Like everything he said and did, the beneficiary was definitively him.

How many generations had we kept that spot a secret from the June-to-August tourists who crowded the lake beach and left their soda cans, candy wrappers, and busted flipflops wherever they landed?

The sale went through with only the tiniest announcement buried in the back pages of the *Gazette*. The caution tape and posted signs were the first any of us heard of it.

Laughing, nervously, we ducked under the tape and made our way down to the hole where we'd swam all our lives. The cops arrived and bull-horned over the river that we were trespassing and had five minutes to vacate or risk arrest.

Men who had grown up there swimming with us turned their faces away when we reminded them of the summers we'd shared. They were just doing their jobs, they said.

The river still belonged to the town and some of us could make it down the opposite river bank, but it was a steep climb and likely to land you splayed and broken on the slate shelf that decked the river, worn smooth by spring and fall floods.

A group of us showed up at the next council meeting and took turns airing our grievances during the public comment portion until we were told our time was up. Two members of the council agreed that something should be done. Three members and the Mayor, who could regularly be found golfing with Jeff Martin during the week when the rest of us were at work, said this was a matter of private property now. They'd followed all required procedures in the sale and if we'd had a problem with it we should have spoken up then.

Three Sundays in a row we protested, crowded by the side of the road with our clever signs and a spirit of camaraderie. The *Gazette* reporter showed up. Took pictures and asked us questions, scribbling in her notebook as we answered, but we never did see a story in the paper.

Our numbers dwindled until it was just me, a handful of folks who protested everything, and the cops telling us once again it was time to move along.

No matter where I was or what I was doing, the swimming hole and Jeff Martin were there in the back of my mind throbbing like a hammer-hit thumb.

It wasn't right.

And there was nothing I could do about it.

My husband, Andy, told me I needed to let it go. We, of all people—two men whose right to love each other out in public hadn't been recognized even half our lives—should know there are bigger worries in the world than the local swimming hole. Racism, sexism, all the isms, and a climate crisis to boot. I shouldn't hold it against the folks who had lost interest, preoccupied with the business of living.

I went to the river, picked my way down the steep side as the sun set and looked for the ghosts of summers past. I imagined myself teaching the child we thought we might adopt how to swim, tossing them over my shoulders, clapping at their underwater somersaults. Giving them the things my father had given me.

Sitting there, head in my hands, I worried Andy was right—this powerless feeling would consume me if I let it and there were far worse wrongs to confront. Better to change myself than give in to the growing resentment of people who didn't care enough to take back what had been given away out from under them.

A voice startled me out of my ruminations.

"Why so down, friend?"

A three-quarters moon had risen over the placid river, lighting the snaking lines of current, wet stone bank, and the leaves of trees lining the top of the gorge on either side. I couldn't spot a soul. A splash in the river caught my attention, and there, in the middle, a salmon the size of a two-year-old swam a lazy circle and asked the question again.

Of course I'd heard of this fish. You can't walk a block in this town without meeting someone who knows someone who almost hooked it, or heard it speak, or watched it leap fifty feet in the air in acrobatic delight. Even my father believed it was as old as the town.

So here was my madness, finally emerging. Well, what can you do but answer when a fish asks a question twice?

I told it my troubles. Explained about Jeff Martin and the town council and the aching maw in my chest for all the friends and neighbors content to let another piece of what should be ours be pirated off by a handful of people.

The fish dipped under the water and I thought I had bored it, but then its head reappeared. "You're a good egg, friend," it said, "so I'm going to do you a solid. A good egg for a good egg." It laughed at its joke in a voice like a hard summer rain. It rolled over, water shimmering off its moon-silvered scales, and popped a small shining orb out of its vent. With a flick of its tail, it lobbed the egg over to me. It glowed orange in my hand, no bigger than a pea. "In three days, when the moon is full, make a wish and eat that." The salmon swam a circle and again came to a stop. "All the usual reminders about being careful what you wish for. You only get the one." And with that it swam off.

I carried the egg home, cradled in my palm, and not knowing what else to do with it, I filled a glass with water and dropped it in.

I told Andy my story and he peered at the little glob at the bottom of the glass. He put the back of his hand up to my forehead. I shrugged him off.

"I'm feeling fine."

"Okay," he said in that way that meant *if you say so*, and asked me what I was going to wish for. I shrugged again and he left me in the kitchen, watching the egg do nothing.

Over the next three days I imagined all manner of wicked ends for Jeff Martin as I worked. If not death, then public humiliations that left him impoverished. In my kinder moods, I considered wishing him a change of heart. A Scroogening. But wasn't there always another Jeff Martin, waiting to take his place?

I thought of personal gain—a windfall of money that would set Andy and I up for life. But then I would be the Jeff Martin, wouldn't I?

On the third night, when the moon rose full and gleaming, I stood on our front lawn and wished the wish of my heart: that good people believed they could make a difference if they tried. I drank the glass of water, the glowing egg sliding over my tongue and down my throat.

I slipped into bed and apologized to Andy for not wishing something for us.

He laughed, "don't be a fool," and kissed me until we were peeling each other's sweats off in the dark.

In the morning, I walked down to the diner for a cup of coffee before work, hoping to find the world changed.

But it was just as it had been the morning before. The *Gazette* followed a developer looking to tear down waterfront buildings and put up luxury condos along the lake. Old white men grumbled at the counter about immigrants taking away jobs, and when I got to work the foreman told our crew we'd have to put in extra hours to make sure the plumbing was roughed in on schedule, but we'd be shorted hours next week so the company didn't have to pay overtime.

Frustrated and exhausted, I got home no longer furious only with Jeff Martin and the people who wouldn't stand up to him, but with myself, for having hoped. Color drained out of the world. Everywhere I looked were signs of the inevitability of everything crumbling to shit.

Andy tried to cheer me, but most evenings ended with me

scrolling through the news, finding proof of all the terrible things in the world and the myriad ways people make each other suffer. I had been earnest and optimistic and what had it gotten me? Nothing but a broken heart.

My neighbors were right. Better to tend to your own affairs and hope the burning world arrived at your doorstep last.

Three weeks into my festering, I arrived home to find Andy sitting at the kitchen table, a stack of papers in front of him. I eyed them as I bent to kiss him and he nodded for me to sit down. He handed a page over to me, a yellow stick-on arrow pointing to a signature line, "Sign there."

"Wha—"

"Just sign."

He was trying to play it serious, like he was in the law office where he worked as a paralegal and I was some client in a suit and tie. But you don't spend fifteen years with a person and not know when they're buzzing to tell you something, so I played along.

I signed three different papers before he hit me with the sidelong smile—his charming snaggletooth crooked and jaunty—that first caught my attention all those years ago. He unfolded a surveyor's map, smoothed it across the table. There was Jeff Martin's house, devil horns drawn out of the roof and a fish penciled in the swimming hole. I followed Andy's finger down to a spot marked with an X.

"About seventy feet south of the swimming hole, the Jenkin's property line starts." He pointed to a spot where the river swung a wide arc away from Valley Road and back towards Banks Road before tumbling down a series of small waterfalls out into the inlet and beyond that, the lake. "Liza has agreed to deed access rights for this portion of land," he circled a rectangle formed by dotted lines, "to the Friends of the River. A nonprofit of which you and I are the founding members. It's steep, but you can build a good set of stairs that would do the trick and then it's just a matter of walking up the bank," his finger trailed back up to the swimming hole.

The world was still on fire, the wealthy were still fucking over as many people as they could, and all manner of horrible shit still needed to be torn down. But look at this man and how he loved me.

I started on the stairs that weekend, clearing a path through the brush and saplings from the street to the cliff edge. About an hour into my work Liza Jenkin's daughter, home from college, arrived with a tool belt slung over her shoulder and a cooler of cold drinks. By lunch, three more neighbors had come to lend a hand.

We worked every Saturday for a month, our numbers growing so large that half of us were just standing around offering encouragement and memories of summers past (somebody's story of a talking fish got us all sharing our own).

Where one person's knowledge faltered—the sturdiest way to anchor the stairs to the rock face, where to get the best price on this material or that—another stood up and offered what they could.

When it was finished we made our way up to the swimming hole, laughing and whooping, our voices amplified off the gorge walls. We cannonballed, or waded in, or sat on the rock-shelf and dangled our toes, and no matter how many police cars Martin called they couldn't stop our jubilee.

E. C. Barrett (she/they) writes folk horror, fabulism and dark speculative fiction. She is or has been an academic, journalist, bookseller, editor, and obituary writer. A Clarion West graduate, E. C. has stories in *Bourbon Penn*, *Baffling Magazine* and elsewhere. E. C. is queer, neurodivergent, and enjoys more maker hobbies than is entirely practical. ecbarrett.com

The Air Will Catch Us

Rajiv Moté

My granddaughter Nisha bounces on the tips of her toes, with flutter kicks in between, a hummingbird barely touching the sidewalk. I adjust the rebreather plugged into my nostrils and push myself forward. Keeping up with her has gotten harder, not just because of my age. Walking is different now. The air resists my habitual gait. Little hops lift me into the thickened atmosphere that slows my return to Earth. It's undignified, but it's past time I got used to this. I'm not *that* old. I bob along after her.

"Not too far," I call. Talking is different too. It takes more effort, timing it with the rebreather. The sounds distort, vowels overwhelming consonants in the heavy air. I have to listen carefully to understand people. Nisha, considerate of my limitations, gives me a thumbs-up. The playground is close, but I grew up not trusting the world. I've watched it change along apocalyptic predictions, down to the air getting hotter, wetter, and thicker every year. And stranger changes, that no one predicted, overwrote the science I learned in school. It's literally a different world than the one I grew up in. I won't trust it with Nisha, unsupervised. While my son and daughter-in-law are at work, the responsibility is mine.

Plots of kudzu line the sidewalk, taller than Nisha. She turns the corner. I quicken my bobs, sucking air through the rebreather with the hollow sound of a patient in a hospital. The kudzu of my childhood was engineered into a kind of terrestrial kelp, with broad leaves undulating in the thickened breeze. Tiny creatures like fish dart among the fronds. The kudzu still tries to spread over everything, but it traps pollutants in nodules that bud like cancer along its stalks. Rebreathers kept the cancer from my generation's bodies. Kudzu keeps it from Nisha's. Maybe I don't need a rebreather now, but I'm susceptible to pneumonia and a panicked sense of drowning when the viscous air enters my lungs. My son calls the dry, thin product of the device "nostalgic air." He doesn't care for it.

Privately, I spend some time every day inhaling the unfiltered atmosphere, training myself not to choke. Sometimes I succeed. It's a trust fall into the world. I'm trying.

The playground's plastic and metal equipment is not much different from my own childhood's. Nisha has a routine. Even before greeting her friends, she scrambles up a ladder and crawls the monkey bars, skipping every other bar. From the last bar she launches herself into space. *The air will catch her.* I don't wait underneath like I used to, but I don't sit down on a bench until she lands on the web of ropes and climbs to a platform.

"You have kids here?" the young mom next to me asks kindly. An unused rebreather is clipped to her shoulder. The kids don't need them, their parents have them "just in case," and their grandparents suck on them like life support. Fashion across the generations.

"Granddaughter," I say, gesturing to Nisha.

"Those two are mine," she says, pointing at a pair of boys, a few years older than Nisha, doing their best to hurl each other, and all comers, off the highest platform. "We used to go to a different park, but this one's actually closer."

I correctly guess they go to Nisha's school, and we talk about homework, teachers, and activities. She's patient as I time my words with the rebreather.

I hear shouting from the playground equipment as if through water. A boy sails over a platform's railing. I can't tell if he was thrown by my bench-mate's boys or jettisoned himself. All the adults watch. None rise to their feet. Kids fly now, but I'm the only one still with a helicopter instinct. I grip the bench and keep my seat. The hiss of my rebreather is fast and shallow. *The air will catch him.* It's like a prayer. The boy somersaults in slow motion, somehow landing on his feet. He bounces and is airborne again, climbing the ropes onto the platforms.

"I'll never get used to that," I say.

"My mother says one never stops worrying."

Her *mother* says that. I suppose it's true. Maybe every generation looks askance at the wonders of the next, afraid to trust them.

I'm embarrassed and irritated by the sound of my breathing. I'm no invalid. As casually as I can manage, I pull the rebreather from my nostrils. I inhale a thick, wet deluge, and manage not to cough. My chest expands. I'm not drowning. I let it out, and bring it back.

Nisha isn't roughhousing. She's talking with girls her age, their voices distorted by the atmospheric soup. But at any moment they could fling themselves from a ladder.

Would you jump off a roof if your friends did? My parents asked me that.

I would if it looked fun, I didn't dare reply.

How the world has changed.

And it does look fun.

I'm on my feet. I don't remember rising. I step onto the ladder rung and pull myself up. This movement is familiar, easier than walking. I'm not as strong anymore, but now I'm buoyant. The strange science that resists me walking also holds me up. The young parents watch with amusement, not worry. They've learned to trust the world. Can I?

I crawl the bars like my granddaughter, every other one, building momentum in slow motion. I grip the last bar with both hands and kick as though swimming, which I haven't done in years. My body remembers.

I launch myself into space.

Rajiv Moté is a writer and software professional living in Chicago with his wife, daughter, and a tiny dog. He writes an epic fantasy column for Dragonmount.com and his stories appear in *Cast of Wonders*, *Diabolical Plots*, *Escape Pod*, and other publications. He can be found on Twitter at @RajivMote and on his website at https://rajivmote.wordpress.com/.

The Split-in-Half Lumberjacks

Sam Claussen

A lumberjack has accidently sawn through his friend;
this sort of thing happens quite frequently. But there is
plenty of wood one might use for their coffins, collected
from a rainforest stripped for its crude oil. Incidentally,
this provides plenty of barren soil for one to bury them:
the split-in-half lumberjacks, interred in a felled mausoleum.

Sam Claussen is a fortunate father, humbled husband, and weary writer from Des Moines, Iowa. Tweet your favorite example of #WordArt to @writeclaussen.

Aftermath

Virginia Boudreau

"There's no fixing this."
My grandmother waves at the tv.
Polar bears are stranded on a shrinking ice floe.
I shut my eyes.

I meet with a student.
She's dealing with an anxiety disorder.
Her brown eyes pool with tears.
"Sometimes it can seem all too much, you know?"
I tell her that just showing up every day is an act of courage.

News coverage of Hurricane Fiona floods the screen.
Huge tracts of PEI shoreline have been devoured by the sea.
Scant sand is littered with spewed remains.
Islanders survey the wreckage with horror and wobbly resolve.

A weary fisherman shakes his head.
"There's no fixing this. It's just too much."

Virginia Boudreau is a retired teacher who makes her home on the south shore of Nova Scotia, Canada. When not at her keyboard, she'll usually be found in her garden or at the shore. Her poetry and prose have been published in a wide variety of international literary venues including *Palette Poetry*, *Grain*, *Westerly*, *Sylvia Magazine*, *The Last Stanza* and *League of Canadian Poets*. Environmental poetry has appeared in: *Revolute*, *Claw and Blossom*, *UnderStorey*, *House of Zolo Press*, and *Little Somethings*.

the world as it is

Sera Gamble

when you realize there's nothing
you can do,
your limbs fill with light.
you rise above lands
cordoned off like VIP areas.
watch the tide swell
over the sweet bodies
of dead bees, smoke
the last air, crown
yourself in final
trees, set yourself
on fire.

Sera Gamble's poems have appeared in publications such as *Birdcoat Quarterly*, *Typehouse*, *Tinderbox*, *Sky Island Journal*, *Lit Angels,* and *Nine Mile Magazine*. She also writes film and television; most recently, she co-created the TV series *You* and *The Magicians*. Sera is a first-generation American living in Los Angeles.

Icediver

Ruth Joffre

Nothing at the bottom of the ocean bothers her. Nothing natural, that is. On a repair job in the Bering Sea last month, she encountered a lost Japanese spider crab hiking back to the Pacific, following a straight line of radiant heat from the subsea fiber-optic cable she had been dispatched to splice together at a break point. As she stripped the cut cables, the spider crab passed overhead in slow motion, its serene, ponderous movements giving her a chance to study the white ridges of its abdomen and the pinched joints of its legs, which towered over her, much longer than she was tall; harder, too, its reddened carapace reminding her of the skeletons of repair robots designed to scuttle into air ducts and reactor cores to perform dangerous maintenance. Her repair jobs usually mean descending to between 5,000 to 10,000 feet below sea-level—at a depth where the extreme water pressure would collapse a human's lungs. When she dives, her lungs compress, pushing all oxygen into the bloodstream to dissolve. Her gills then open, three delicate slits at the base of her throat opening on each side of her neck to allow seawater to flow over the filaments and oxygenate the blood. Once submerged, her adaptable body temperature and webbed phalanges enable her to live quite comfortably underwater for days or weeks at a time—a capability telecoms were quick to capitalize upon when her species of deep sea dwellers first surfaced about a century ago. Now, Vira jumps at every job opportunity, knowing they will be few and far between.

Her last job was a month ago. Before that, she was living lean off a gig in February.

It's August now, and tourist season in Alaska is less than a month from closing.

Her mother will be out of work again soon.

On the way to pick her mother up from her seasonal job at Kodiak Gulf Floor Tours, Inc., Vira recalculates her September–May budget: $600 per month for her share of the rent for a small two-bedroom apartment she still shares with her mom, $300 per month in student loan payments, $120 per month on average for cell service and the extra data she'll need once she goes over their low limits, another $100 per month to help with gas and car insurance, and about $200 per month for groceries to supplement all the fish she caught, dried, or froze for winter. By her calculations, she has less than $400 left over after bills and necessities to splurge on little gifts for herself, but chances are good her mom will burn right through that with something or other—parking tickets, bail, yet another get-rich-quick scheme that will inevitably blow up in her face.

"Maybe Dave will have something for me," she mutters, pulling into the parking lot.

Once parked, she takes a deep breath, reminding herself, *Be nice. You need the money.*

Dave picks up after barely one ring. "Well, well, well if it isn't my favorite mermaid!"

"I prefer the term sirenx," she reminds him, banging her head inaudibly against the rest.

"Right. Sorry about that." She can hear him wince in discomfort. "So, what's up, Vira?"

She tries not to sound desperate. "I was just calling to see if you have any jobs for me."

He hums, clicking through company portals at his desk to check. "Nothing right now."

His elongated vowels make her think he is hiding something, so she presses. "What about next month? I heard about the plan to build a diverse fiber line on the north side of the Aleutians. Not sure where that is in the process, but I would be happy to install the branching units, like last time." Her head tilts into a joking shrug, even though he can't see her on the phone. "Lord knows they'll need a bunch of branches to hit all the communities on the chain."

"Tell me about it." As a former resident of False Pass, he allows himself a brief moment of bitterness over the delay in extending fiber to his community from the original line festooned on the south side of the Aleutian Chain. "But that project is still in permitting. We're not planning to lay cables until next spring at the earliest. And that's probably aggressive. You know how these things go. It could be five years before anything moves forward. Or six months. Who knows?"

Her forehead rests, dejected, on the steering wheel, but she forces herself to sound casual, like someone who doesn't need this. "I hear ya. Keep me in mind when you do get there, okay?"

"Absolutely. You're at the top of my list, so it's good to know you're interested."

She swallows a lump in her throat. "Definitely. Just tell me when and where."

"Will do. And I'll let you know if anything comes up in the meantime. . . ."

His trailing period makes her think there may be something else, so Vira pauses a second, indulging in the fantasy that he will fill the silence with a job, but she gives up and says goodbye. With a sigh, she hangs up, muttering, "It was a long shot, anyway," into the blank, shining face of the smartphone. Her mother's last tour is scheduled to return in about ten minutes, so Vira leaves her phone in the glove compartment and heads down to the docks in her bathing suit. At this time of year, the water temperatures around Kodiak hover at about 55°F, though they get warmer each passing summer. Most casual swimmers on the shore still wear trunks, but tourists with weighted boots and full-body pressure suits venture farther, with the help of licensed guides, into the frigid depths of the Gulf of Alaska.

Her mother Bárbara is one of the tour guides. Just part sirenx by way of her grandmother on her father's side, Bárbara cannot dive to the same depths as Vira, whose father, a full-blooded sirenx, passed down his gills and compressible lungs before disappearing back under the surface. On the job, Bárbara wears a supplemental oxygen tank, but none of the high-tech gear her clients require. Her uniform consists of a bikini top and a flowing skirt made from seaweed so that when she swims around, her long hair flows behind her in the current, and the tourists think, "Wow, she looks like a mermaid!" A lot of the online reviews for Kodiak Gulf Floor Tours, Inc. read exactly like that. Every once in a while, someone comments, "Would've been better if she wore a tail."

When Vira arrives, her mother hugs her close and whispers, "This is a testy bunch."

With a fake smile for the tourists, Vira asks, "Want me to show off a bit?"

"Could you? I want to end the season on a high note."

Everyone is already looking at Vira by then and pointing their underwater cameras at her. One arm propped on a signpost labeled Gray Whale Watchtower, she asks, “Y’all want a show?” She knows the helmets of their suits have noise-cancelling technology, in order to prevent auditory overstimulation from the engines of cruise ships and recreational boats sailing overhead. Still, the sight of her mouth moving underwater impresses them, and they can tell they are in for a treat. She waves them closer, smiling, then lifts off the gulf floor, twirling and somersaulting like a synchronized swimmer in an Esther Williams movie as their shutters click in unison. Earlier in the season, she might have been joined by gray whales on their migratory path to the Bering Sea. Today, the tourists must settle for some playful sea otters who join her on a lark, their long, sleek bodies corkscrewing through the water.

Sometimes, Vira thinks she has spent her entire life sitting in the audience, waiting, while other people pursue their dreams. As a child, she passed entire summers hanging out on Kodiak’s beaches, scanning the horizon for signs of her father, whose human name was Mateo; her mother never did learn his given name or the location of that underwater city she believes he returned to not long after Vira’s first birthday. “I got the sense that life down there was rather turbulent,” she said once, “and that people back home were expecting him to return and help fix things.” Maybe, once the troubles were resolved, he would return, and they could be a family again—at least, that was what Vira hoped. In her fantasies, her father was a tall, well-insulated man, strong enough to carry her around on his shoulders and yet soft enough to hug her and wish her good luck before a swim meet. In ninth grade, she tried out for the high school swim team, thinking that learning the human swim forms would build her endurance for future trips with her father. But almost as soon as the swim coach spotted her webbed fingers and shuttered gills, all hopes were dashed. It would be unfair, the other parents argued, for their children to compete against a merhuman hybrid. She would always have an advantage, they insisted—just look at those toes! Nevermind that Vira had never swum the butterfly in her life. Only after school, when applying for jobs, were her physical adaptations considered a benefit, not a frightening liability.

Employers love cutting costs. One $15,000 repair job for Vira could easily cost a telecom $400,000 once you account for the cost of dispatching the boats, the fuel, the salaries of the crew members—not to mention the collateral damage to businesses reliant on that connectivity and the environment soaking up all that diesel pollution. How much would you pay a merhuman to solve your problems?

"How would you feel if you paid $1,500 and didn't even get a selfie?" Her mother's boss, Benj, flings this question like mud as he follows Bárbara out the front door of the office. All their customers are gone, their tour gear stowed and credit cards charged so they can return to their big cruise ships and luxury hotel rooms, so now Benj and Bárbara are alone but for an administrative assistant blowing bubbles at the desk and Vira, sitting barefoot on the dock, dipping her toes into the gulf. He opens his hand, almost plaintive. "Just think about it from their perspective."

Bárbara stops halfway down the dock and sighs. "I can't control the whales, Benj."

He smiles like someone who has heard this before and had time to fashion a good counter argument for it. "But you do speak their language," he says, "and you can call to them."

"That only works if they're in range." Her arm sweeps out to point northwest. "Most gray whales are all the way on the other side of the Aleutians by now."

"That may be true, but you could at least call to them. Give the tourists a show."

"They won't be able to hear it, anyway." She leans toward him, tapping the wet hair right above her left ear. "Noise-cancelling technology, remember?"

"Careful, Barb. You already have two strikes against you."

"Come on. Be reasonable, Benj. It's the end of the season."

"And I'm trying to make sure we're all still here next season, okay? It's not like we're the only tourist trap in town. These richie rich tourists expect us to pull out all the stops now." Hands on his hips, he shakes his head and turns away from her, scuffing his shoes on the dock. When he spots Vira, he says, "Now here's someone who knows how to put on a real show. Why don't you come work for me, Vira?"

"I don't know, Benj. Will you give me time off for better-paying temp gigs?"

He pushes his lips together and hums disapproval. "Let me think about it."

Once in the car, her mother says, "Sometimes, this job isn't worth it."

Vira waits for a man with sunblock caked on his nose to pass before turning onto the road toward their apartment building. "Pay's decent. And besides, it's only a couple more weeks; then you can hunker down for the winter and catch up on your shows."

"It can't come quickly enough. I'm so tired of people looking at me. Pointing at me." She hangs her head in her hands, then rubs her eyelids with her fingertips. For her, the transition from blinking underwater to walking around in the bright sun often causes bad headaches. Her hybrid eyes must adjust to that light and pressure, the spherical black lenses able to process much more information on the periphery than the flat lenses of humans. In the past, the difficulty of the transition had caused several car accidents after work. Now, Vira picks her mother up and listens to her vent about work five days a week (six during peak season). Bárbara leans back and sighs with closed eyes. "Sometimes, I wish I could disappear. Or that Benj would disappear."

At a stoplight, Vira studies her mother. "I noticed he called you Barb."

"I hate it when he does that. Like we're friends."

Only after they parked did Vira ask, "What did he mean, two strikes?"

"Oh, don't worry, honey. You know how some men love their power trips."

Her mother always says "some men" in order to exclude Mateo from critiques. Even after twenty-four years of complete silence, she still considers him beyond reproach. "Your father was unfailingly kind," she explained once, when Vira asked the fateful question: *Why? Why would he leave us?* "He wouldn't disappear without a good reason. I bet he's out there right now, planning our reunion." This capacity for selective optimism always surprised Vira, who learned at an early age how to interpret her mother's moods. After a long day she liked to be the first one inside their apartment, so she could settle down alone, removing her shoes and socks and massaging that tender spot between the toes where the boots pinched the webbing. On days like this, Vira lingers outside, checking the air pressure in the tires, chatting with the elderly lesbians who live upstairs, considering whether she might hike across the Pacific like that Japanese spider crab and what the consequences would be if she did.

Half an hour later, she decides to head inside, and that's when she finds it: the missed call from Dave, followed by a message saying, *Call me back? I think I've got a job for you....*

Nothing is without risk. Her work is no exception. Once, on a rare multi-week contract to repair fiber-optic spurs off a ring around the North Slope, she dipped under an iceberg floating in the Chukchi Sea and met with the gaping maw of a polar bear hunting in the freezing waters. In a sprint, that sleek white bear was almost as fast, but not nearly as well fed, and she was able to pull away from the mother, whose cub huddled on a nearby iceberg, gnawing at its paws. From a safe distance, Vira watched the mother surface, sopping wet fur hanging low and thin, like the threadbare strands of seaweed in her mother's work skirt. In emergencies like that, Vira had been instructed to press a gray button in the locator device on her wrist, which served as GPS, beacon, and—if she happened to be in range of a cell tower—a short-range communicator. Some lawyers in tailored suits had devised this precaution to protect her employers from liability, but in reality, such a device was of no use in dangerous situations. A predator could eat, digest, and excrete her before a medevac or rescue crew could reach her. Functionally, the device served one purpose: to alert the company to hire another contractor to complete the job. Thus far, Vira has never pressed that button.

"This job might change that," Dave warns on a call. "It's the riskiest gig I've ever seen."

"That's why you're paying me triple," Vira says. She has already signed the contract; this pre-departure check-in is just a formality, a means of assessing her mental fitness before he signs off on the paperwork, authorizing payment of $50,000 on completion of the assignment.

His breaths whistle slightly, like a deflating balloon. "Are you sure you'll be okay?"

"You know as well as I do I'm the only one who has a hope of surviving at that depth."

"Still. 15,000 feet sounds like a lot. I keep picturing you getting crushed or eaten by some deep-sea leviathan." His voice trembles dramatically, as if narrating the trailer of a black and white B-movie with rudimentary special effects.

"You know my people come from the ocean, right? We've lived there for millennia."

"Technically, we all come from primordial oceans. That's evolution. But this is 2036."

"Yeah, and rent's only getting more expensive. I need this job to pay my internet bill."

He snorts at the astronomical cost of connectivity in rural Alaska. "Good luck with that."

"Does that mean I'm cleared?" She crosses her fingers as she waits for him to say yes.

"Plane'll be there in the morning. 8 AM sharp. It'll take you as far as Chirikof. After that, you'll be on your own." He dwells on this point for longer than she does. "Try to make it back to Kodiak in one piece, okay? I'd hate to have to replace you."

What she promises him and what she promises her mother and herself are entirely different things. Her mother would like her to take this opportunity to seek information about her father and the mysterious city he called home. Bárbara would have her ask each passing mammal if they've seen a merman fitting his description. "About six foot three, brown skin, hair pulled up in a topknot and tied with a ribbon. Once went by the name of Mateo and married a merhuman of mixed Bolivian and white descent—might've talked at length about her legs. Ringing any bells?" Nothing would embarrass Vira more. Beyond fixing the break, her plan for this excursion was simple: explore. Familiarize herself with the terrain. Figure out whether she could survive, not just at this depth, but with the creatures who called it home. Would her lungs implode? Would the bioluminescent squid enchant her into making a home underwater?

A part of her longs for it: the quiet, the freedom from human life.

She barely says a word on the flight to Chirikof. She cannot bear it.

Only after the seaplane drops her off and coasts to shore to refuel does she feel safe. Now the hard work can begin. First, she checks her GPS coordinates, noting her latitude and longitude (55°43'58.7"N 155°31'11.1"W). Her target is approximately thirty-five miles south, near the dark mouth of the Aleutian Trench, where a subsea fiber line connecting Seward, Alaska to Hokkaido, Japan had been placed only nine months prior. *No wonder the company wants to keep this repair quick and quiet*, she thinks, descending into the pitch-black waters of the North Pacific. Here, she wears a full body swimsuit reinforced with Kevlar to protect against shark attacks, a sensor array capable of detecting motion within 150 feet and flashing light at frequencies known to repel apex marine predators, and that all but useless monitor on her wrist, which she continues wearing only because she hates littering and would not leave this trash for her people to clean up.

At no point during the descent does she expect to meet one of her kind.

It comes as a surprise. A flutter of fin on the bottom of her foot. A nibble on her shoulder as she follows the line of broken subsea cable down the jagged slopes of the Aleutian Trench. She flails at the touch and briefly loses her footing. It takes her a moment to calm down.

"Who's there?" She flicks on the floodlight of her headlamp. "Show yourself."

On her second survey of the area, she spots a merperson poking her head out from behind a towering rock spire that may once have been a volcanic vent. With her body hidden by the rock and her hair pulled back into a net adorned with a single seashell, she resembles a dreamy singer-songwriter posing for an album cover in the nineties. "Deep apologies for attempting to eat you," she says. "Your suit makes you look like a seal."

"No worries. Just don't try it again, okay?"

"Okay. My English name is Pod. Do you like the sound? Pod."

"I do," Vira says, dimming the light, "but it's not my place to judge your name."

Pod comes forward to inspect Vira and her lamp. "What name have you chosen?"

“My name was given to me. It’s in honor of Viracocha—an ancient Incan deity.”

“He who rose from the lake and brought the light,” Pod says, as if recalling a textbook.

“How do you know him? I didn’t think that the northern and southern merpeople talked.”

“We rarely do, but my teacher told us all about him.” She circles Vira, studying the straps on her waist, the translucent case of the sensor array that knew before Vira did that Pod was not a predator. She appears to delight in the shortness of Vira’s hair and the way it sways in the waters, like stubby strands of brown kelp. Her eyes flash with revelation. “Have you met my teacher? He spent time on land.”

“Probably not. Most of the merpeople I’ve met work for fisheries, reducing bycatch.”

Pod sulks a bit and then fixes Vira with wide, iridescent eyes. “Can I trust you?”

This is it, Vira thinks. *I’m finally going to visit an underwater city.* “Yes.”

“Good. Now, turn off your lamp,” Pod says, offering a hand. In the dark, she guides Vira, warning her about the spines of snailfish, the plumes of hydrothermal vents, the red tentacles of a giant squid passing overhead, its angry black eye fixed on something far off in the distance. First, they walk down the slope, tracing the line of cut fiber. Then, when the rock falls away under them in a sharp cliff, the women begin to swim, following the curve of the cable as it disappears into a recessed cave in the wall of the trench. Someone had to have brought the cable there, Vira thinks. Someone cut it on purpose. All concern as to why dissipates after Pod leads her through a tunnel, into the hollowed mountain she calls home. From a ledge, they look out at a gleaming city full of elaborate spires and shimmery sea glass, illuminated with electricity generated by hydrothermal vents. It expands before them for what seems like miles. “Welcome,” Pod says, “to Atxuni.”

In one of the few photographs of her father in existence, Vira is still a newborn. A yellow baby blanket swaddles her, so soft and fuzzy that it makes her look like a baby duck with her feet tucked under her feathers for warmth. Her eyes are open, their mottled irises pointed up at Mateo smiling down at her, his face tilted at an angle she cannot remember. Her only memories of her father have been manufactured from photographs like that, with the camera tilted, the light shifted in her mind, so she can believe she was precious to him. *He loved you*, her mother always insisted, but even as a child she picked up on the use of the past tense, as if love was like oxygen: essential on land but quick to dissolve once he slipped under the surface. All her life, even during the summers when she waited for him on the beach, she harbored a bitterness toward him, a hard, unyielding part of herself that accepted none of her mother's high-minded excuses for his sudden departure. *His people needed him. He must have been a great leader, or maybe a doctor.* Early in the tour of Atxuni, Vira asks Pod if she knows anyone by his description, anyone who mentioned becoming a father on the surface, but Pod says no—to her knowledge, no one has left the city for the surface in more than a generation. "Of course, this is not the only city in the trench. There are dozens of others. You should ask there, too."

"Maybe I will," Vira says, knowing this will be a journey for another day.

"Feather might be able to give you a map. Or at least point you in the right direction."

Feather, thinks Vira, imagining a flying fish. "Has everyone here taken English names?"

"Just Feather's students. He came here on an exchange program from one of the Southern Water Cities. He used names to teach us other languages and dialects. In our English unit, no one liked the traditional human names he suggested, so we all decided to invent our own." She rattles off some of the names: *Flame. Rattle. Disco. Optic.*

"I wonder what I would have picked," Vira muses, staring up at a winding spire.

"Ooo, let me guess." Pod considers her for a long moment before saying, "Green tea."

With a laugh, Vira shakes her head. "I was thinking something like Ice. Or—Iceberg."

"Iceberg. Like the lettuce." Vira grimaces, but Pod beams.

"Ready to meet Feather?"

Before Vira can respond, Pod parts a curtain of seaweed doubling as a gate and shows her Atxuni's political province, which stretches out before them for the equivalent of several big city blocks before extending up the face of a cliff in five towers carved directly into the rock. Each of the towers rises a hundred or more stories, recalling the skyscrapers Vira has seen only on screen (Kodiak being a relatively short, modest town in comparison to, say, Chicago). At the base of the third tower, Pod says, "We'll have to swim to reach my office." In the water, her body is sinuous and patient, pausing frequently to give Vira time to gaze about in wonder and ask questions, such as: "What are the signs on the sides of the towers?" Pod translates: "These indicate the level and the associated conclave and council. For example, this is the Subduction Refugee and Climate Crisis Conclave. And these next ten levels are the Houses of Grievances and Amends. You might have to visit these to figure out who cut your fiber line and how to fix it."

Treading water, Vira asks, "Should we go now? Make sure this gets on the docket?"

This word, "*docket*", puzzles Pod, and she shakes her head. "No, there is never a line."

"Oh," Vira says, with a self-conscious laugh, then follows Pod up to her office within the Conclave of Edification and Inquiry. Nothing inside the building reminds Vira of an office on the surface—those sad gray boxes people fold themselves into day after day, year after year, as if production was the main goal of their one precious life. Where she expects desks, whiteboards, and rolling chairs, she sees glass bubbles large enough to fit two people, each one outfitted with a screen whose liquid surface ripples like plasma. Most lie dormant, but one displays images on it, which she realizes are projected by a device that resembles the horn of a gramophone. From this, she detects a strange, complex hum, never repeating, impossible to predict. Out of curiosity, Vira calls out to Pod, asking, "What is this?"

Helplessness subsumes Pod's face as she searches for a suitable word. "A . . . telephone?"

"But it sends images," Vira says. She kneels down to better study the mechanics.

"Yes. It . . . encodes and decodes them." Pod points to a

resonant tube. "Here."

"Ingenious. It's like our fiber-optic cable, but with directed sound waves."

An unfamiliar male voice behind her says, "An apt observation."

Feather. Pod hugs him and says, "I am glad you are still here. I brought a visitor."

"Hello," Feather says, extending a hand to Vira in a motion that feels novel and practiced, like something he learned in a sociology class about surface-dwellers. "Where are you from?"

"Kodiak." Uncertain if he knows it, she elaborates, "About 200 miles from here."

"You are practically a local, then. Is this your first time to one of our cities?"

Before Vira can nod, Pod interjects, "I found her near the cut fiber line."

No part of this startles him, Vira notes. He says, "I figured they would send someone."

"And here I am." She flaps her arms at her sides, feeling very ordinary, the exact opposite of magnificent in this remarkably shining city. Now that she's here, Vira realizes she would have preferred come to Atxuni in her own time, on her own terms, without the logo of a multi-million-dollar business emblazoned on a device on her wrist; but that isn't the case, and she still has a job to do. She hopes they both understand this. "You wouldn't happen to know who cut the fiber and why, would you? I only ask because they sent me to fix it, and if I do and it gets cut again they're going to get mad, and that could be very bad for me and for the secrecy of this place."

"We are not a secret. We are just too expensive to invade. But your point is taken."

"So . . . do you know who cut the fiber line?" She suspects he never gets his hands dirty.

"I do. Our team worked with engineers from the Conclave of Machinery and Innovation." He explains at a high level the desire to explore methods of transmitting data over long distances, such as the many thousands of miles between Atxuni and the Southern Pacific Water Cities. "We expect this capability will be critical when the climate refugee crisis accelerates."

"And since light travels faster than sound, you want to switch to our fiber technology."

"No." He says this in the firm, decisive tone of one who has already secured consensus in that regard and will not reconsider the matter. "But we were glad of the opportunity to study your technology up close. Until recently, most fiber lines avoided this trench, making a controlled and secure study untenable. This new line allowed us to learn much in a short period of time."

"Does that mean your study is complete? I can repair the line?"

"By all means," he says, with a slight bow of the head.

"No offense, but: do you have the authority to approve that?"

Feather and Pod exchange quizzical looks. "I am the Primary of the Conclave," he begins by way of explaining his position. "To you, that would be akin to the head of a major department in your nation's government."

"Like the Secretary of Education."

"Precisely."

"But you said another conclave was involved?"

"In cases of collaboration and partnership, the one speaks for the whole."

What she says is, "Okay," but what she thinks to herself is, *That sounds like a really good way to silence dissent and create a false sense of unity*. That does not seem to be Feather's intent, but she is wary of believing Atxuni to be perfect, idealizing a place she has never lived because it appears to have solved problems no one can even be bothered to acknowledge in her society. She sighs at the thought of going back, but it must be done. She has a job to do, but she doesn't know how to say goodbye. "Well, that solves that. No need to go to the House of Grievances, after all."

"Oh no." Pod's voice deflates with disappointment. "You're not leaving already?"

"It's a long swim back. I should probably just fix the line and get going."

"No, no," Feather and Pod say in unison. He assures Vira, "We can speak to the Conclave of Transportation about chartering a submarine. It will cut your journey down considerably."

"Are you sure? That sounds expensive. And it's really not necessary. I can manage."

"We insist," Pod says. "You are our cousin from the surface. You should see the city."

"And I know a team of engineers who would love to talk to a technician of your caliber."

"I'm basically a mechanic with strong lungs," she says, knowing they will protest, feeling perhaps for the first time in her life that she might be more than just a telecom tech, a gig worker, perpetually at the mercy of the economy and the vicissitudes of executive decision making. Here in Atxuni, her unique talents matter more than they ever have before and perhaps ever will again. She agrees to speak with the civic engineers about their plans for longitudinal transmission tubes. Over dinner, they discuss fault lines, hydrothermal capture, the manner in which kelp or seaweed can be processed and extruded into delicate beds of noodles for the raw fish slices served to them on plates of smoothed sea glass. Floating down an alley, marveling at the intricate tile mosaics of squid and spiny dogfish, she finds herself thinking, *I could live here*, then stopping herself with a familiar question: *What about Bárbara?*

On the submarine ride to Kodiak, she studies the holographic map Feather gave her of the Northern Pacific Water Cities, which stretch across the vast expanse of the ocean from Tokyo in the west to Panama City in the east, from the Aleutian Trench in the north to the equator dividing north and south. It would take years—decades, even—to search these Water Cities for her father Mateo, and there would be no guarantee of finding him. She could be in the same city as him, rest on a bench as he swims overhead mere feet away, and still miss him. He could be in Atxuni right now, going on with his life without her. Her father, the abandoner. Only after Feather handed her the map Pod promised did Vira realize part of her was invested in the fantasy that Pod was going to accidentally reintroduce her to Mateo; that theirs was to be a narrative of coincidence, reunion, maybe even forgiveness—but that is not this story, she admits. That is just her seeking an answer to a question asked long ago: *Why did he leave me?*

Her submarine pilot asks a better question: "Are you planning to return to Atxuni?"

"I think so. I'm not sure when, though. I have a lot of things to take care of."

He hums his understanding. "Is life on the surface very complicated?"

"Very." Not wanting to think about it, she turns to watch the submarine's mechanical fins gliding effortlessly though the cold water. Forward and back, forward, back. Unlike human-made submarines, with their tin-can aesthetic, mersubmarines were shaped like humpback whales, with extended pectoral fins and a soft, slumped belly, allowing the sub to curve and to circulate water. Like most mertech, the sub was powered by a combination of trapped hydrothermal energy and a perpetual circulation machine activated by ocean currents. Out of the water, the sub, like the holo map Feather provided, would cease to function. She zooms in again on the Aleutian Trench cities and asks the pilot, "Are all water cities as beautiful as Atxuni?"

"All the ones I've been to. Some even more so."

"Which one would you recommend visiting?"

"For you? Qirz. It's a domed city with waterfalls and beautiful gardens; their Conclave of Hybridity has done wondrous things marrying mertech and human mechanical engineering."

"It sounds like they should be overseeing the longitudinal transmission project."

"Oh, all the trench cities work together. But Atxuni was closest to the fiber."

"Makes sense," she says, though she has more questions than time to ask them.

The pilot pulls up in front of Gray Whale Watchtower, and Vira has to say goodbye.

Almost as soon as she sets foot on Kodiak, dread seeps into her heart, heavy and familiar. How will she explain her experience in Atxuni to Bárbara? And should she even try? Her mother cannot survive at such depths. She cannot swim that trench or embark on an endless quest to find Mateo—that gilded, glorious image she manufactured of him so that he could never possibly live up to her expectations. Still, if there was any possibility of reuniting with her long lost lover, Bárbara would have taken it without question. On bad nights when Vira was just a kid and had to peel her mother out of a depression in the couch, Bárbara would sneer, "I shoulda sent you to live at your cousin's in the Lower 48; then I wouldn't be in this mess." This mess meaning the trappings of paying for an apartment and a mouth to feed, plus whatever trouble she had gotten herself into drinking or gambling. If Bárbara knew Vira had a connection to Atxuni, she would try her best to capitalize on it. Arrange submarine tours. Bring back mertech.

No, decides Vira. She will not tell Bárbara what happened.

Before heading home, she stops at Dave's office to return her locator device and check on throughput post-repair. "Another excellent job, Vira—we're back up to a total of five terabits per second," he boasts, pointing to real-time data visualizations on his screen. Hair still dripping over her right shoulder, she watches Dave perform the final tests to confirm satisfactory completion of the job. While he completes the requisite forms, he asks a question for which she has prepared an answer: "So, what do you think did it?"

"Earthquake debris. You know how volatile the Aleutians are. Surprised you built there."

"Yeah, well." He shrugged, filing the paperwork away. "That's above my paygrade."

With a laugh, she says goodbye with a wave. "Call me next time it breaks."

He nods and salutes her with two fingers. "You got it."

Outside, Vira pauses to enjoy the warm sun on her dry clothes and the $50,000 super rush job rate soon to hit her bank account. With that kind of money, she could take the rest of the year off and explore the other trench cities on Feather's holo map. As she walks home in the perpetual August light she thinks, *I just might.* Why not? She's young—just twenty-three going on twenty-four—and she's grown tired of Kodiak, the high cost of milk, the looks white people in particular give her when they notice her gills. For the first time, she thinks she knows what made her father abandon his new family.

He wasn't a hero, she realizes. He just wanted to feel like he belonged.

Ruth Joffre is the author of the story collection *Night Beast*. Her work has appeared or is forthcoming in *Lightspeed*, *Nightmare*, *Pleiades*, *khōréō*, *The Florida Review Online*, *Wigleaf*, *Baffling Magazine*, and the anthologies *Best Microfiction 2021 & 2022*, *Unfettered Hexes: Queer Tales of Insatiable Darkness*, and *Evergreen: Grim Tales & Verses from the Gloomy Northwest*.

In Memory of Thwaites Glacier

Ivy Raff

A new oceanographic
ice fades from underneath.
they knew. Tunnels rut
miles of eyeless organisms, carry
of earth to pole. The ice looses
empties itself. Crust crumbles

revelation: glacial
The ocean plumbs deeper than
floor, caverned under
water from belt
its undersides,
into iceberg-speckled sea.

Once the glacier stiffed its lower lip,
Now she slopes,
achievements
loose diamonds
of watery energy inside.
Once bound together
a frozen mountain. Now,
mutinied

rugged
a mother emptynested
into the world
or loose cannons,
Ready to unleash
by millennial ice,
with her child soldiers
the mountain threatens

self-protective.
having sent her
Necklace shattered into
sons with an excess
at a split second
the bergs girded
forcibly
to crash.

Ivy Raff's debut chapbook, *Rooted and Reduced to Dust* (Finishing Line Press, forthcoming 2024), was hailed by Jimmy Santiago Baca as "sensuous, glowing with an undercarriage of mystique." Her poetry appears in *The American Journal of Poetry, Nimrod International Journal,* and *West Trade Review*, among numerous others, and is anthologized in *Spectrum: Poetry Celebrating Identity*. Currently nominated for the *Best of the Net Anthology*, Ivy's work has garnered scholarship support from the Colgate Writers' Conference as well as residencies with Atlantic Center for the Arts and Alaska State Parks. She lives and bakes artisan challah in Northern New Jersey.

Carbon Sink

Colm O'Shea

Slender frogs spring, weightless,
weaving through bog cotton.

Rows of cut turf monuments come to a sheer drop—
the *bog hole*: a cliff of richest fudge
feeding into a red wine gorge, thick with tannins.

Here, all pleasures compress: dull, heavy, glutting.
At this end of the field everything pulls
down with a gravity of its own, draws us
into sumptuous density.

Grant us release from temptation, we say,
burning another sod of ancient peat,
watching smoke calligraphy curl
dense apocalyptic language in the room,
consuming, even as we exhale.

We know not the day nor hour,
but the gorging age will pass.
Our heavy hands will sublimate, spectral fingers
rise, rearrange the carbon letters, re-spell
revelation from the hollow burning bell
As sure as every feast is followed by a fast

the heavens in the hells shall duly shine up-cast.

Colm O'Shea teaches writing at New York University. His monograph, *James Joyce's Mandala*, on sacred/morbid geometry in Joyce's fiction, and *Claiming De Wayke*, his novel about VR addiction during a pandemic, are available to order at colmoshea.com. He also co-hosts The Rescape Project with physical educator Robbie O'Driscoll, where they explore the value of play.

Cantre'r Gwaelod

Elizabeth Wilson Davies

rising again   stumps of oak pine birch willow hazel
emerge from the sand   Noah's trees

their roots stiffened underground   protectors of bones
where families were planted centuries ago
and animal and human footprints remain

scatterings of burnt stones from submerged ancient hearths
revealed by equinoctial tides and storms

the dead stay with us like bruises

well maiden no more   Mererid's plaintive call
reverberates on the wind   lamenting

the sea swell crashing in flooding
Gwyddno's lowlands with featureless water

blurred memories of drunken Siethenyn's cries
ring out as the wild sea swept through open floodgates
covering the contours until each person   each animal   each tree

drowned   hear the watch-tower's bells toll the secrets of the sea
wishing they are unforgotten on the shore

the opaque sky of Ynyslas is engulfed by metallic bird
calls. A print of a small bare foot preserved
in hardened peat endures

this child bore witness to the loss   we too face westwards
into the encroaching sea

rising

Elizabeth Wilson Davies (@LizWilsonDavies) is a poet from Pembrokeshire in west Wales. She has an MA in Creative Writing and a PhD in Post-colonial Literatures and has received mentoring support through the Literature Wales scheme from Welsh poets Samantha Wynne-Rhydderch and Paul Henry. She was awarded a Literature Wales New Writer's Bursary and recently won first prize in the PENfro Literature Festival for her poem 'Heartland'.

A Song for the Selkies

Oyedotun Damilola Muees

The mystery behind humans and their avarice for power is unfathomable. Over the years this enigma has perturbed our hearts; still no answer is readily available. For so long our forefathers have been water nomads, leaving abruptly at the sight of humans and their heavy machineries polluting our waters. It has become a habit for us, expecting them to always invade our homes once we find a new settlement. The aged ones tell us tales of how minelayer and torpedo annihilate our former homes in one strike, sending our loved ones to their early graves.

When we sleep in the deep and calm waters, they come again, encroaching our space without regard for our privacy. We scamper higgledy-piggledy, calling out to our families, carrying only the valuables: totem, spears, trove, and shell pendants. We swim farther, away from the deadly scents of humans. We watch the statues and the tombstones of our ancestors collapse to a second death. Mother says never to look back, all that is destroyed is in the past.

With tears and an unforeseen bleak future we seek for a refuge. Temporarily we find one. Though the constant inclement weather tugs at our hearts, unsolicited fears hold our entire bodies prisoner. It is no surprise that our new home is already inhabited by malevolent merfolk who do not regard that we are both autochthons of the sea. They call us spiteful names, raining invective on the leader of our tribes. It's not our fault that our skins and flippers are in high demand by humans. After much deliberation, they grant us a temporary place to stay. We are reminded of the hegemon in charge. The mermaids scowl at us, repeatedly telling our females to stay clear of their mermen before flipping their iridescent turquoise scaly tails and dragging their mermen away as though they are priceless jewels.

I have no interest in those flirty mermen. All that matters is the safety of my tribe. The first time we saw our hosts in action, they destroyed a caisson with their weapons, leaving the carcass as a souvenir for its human owners. The ways of the merfolk are brutish. Their leader, wielding the trident, had once said, *Humans do not give a fuck about you. Do what you must to survive. They have no regard for your homes.* The humans sent a frogman to ascertain the cause of the damage. He never returned to his people. Our hosts called our attention once they had caught and restrained him. We saw his foot fins, flippers, lying on the ground. Mother charged at him, asking why he killed our kind and used our body parts. What an audacity, we echoed. He drowned after the gas in his air cylinder was exhausted.

In exchange for food and safety, some of us offer ourselves in pleasure to the mermen, stripping our coats to reveal our voluptuous figures for their pleasure. They take us to their chambers and ram us in excitement, not minding some of us are celibate. *We do what must be done to survive.* The oracle's voice reverberates in our subconscious when we permit them entry into our bodies.

Sometimes when the waves become unusually tempestuous, the mermen swim to the surface. We are excited to bask in the stories they tell us of humans. Not all humans are bad, they say, with all manner of sincerity, forgetting they have already told us that humans are terrible. They adorn our necks with tawdry human trinkets, confess their love for us, and take off our skins so they can further dwell in awe of our naked bodies, whether we want them to or not.

One serene afternoon, the sun rises to its highest, beaming and smiling at us while we sit beneath the cerulean water. Little do we know that the rays piercing the depth of the sea are a harbinger telling us to be wary. Human soldiers dive into the water in force, looking for the frogman that we killed. They catch us unprepared, our spears are no match for their assault rifles. Few of us are lucky, swimming fast to safety. After all, that is all we know how to do—run, run, always run.

Perhaps the merfolk are right to have called us a cursed tribe. Our mothers pray fervently to the gods, wishing for a safe home. The gods answer, bringing us to a river devoid of harmful human activities. Aside from the usual fishing of the locals, teenagers swimming before sunset, their actions pose no threat. A few urinate and shit into the water, toss empty bottles of ogogoro into it. This doesn't scare us. We already knew that humans have no respect for nature.

We have no cause to leave our home until a trace of danger raises its ugly head. Deep in the silvery-streaked, not-too-tainted water, we frolic. Tranquility towers higher than the seamount. The mollusks treat us to a melody that also serenades the sea anemones. The image of the sun is distorted from our location, but we can tell it's happy we finally have a safe haven. Even the heavy downpour graces our homes with warmth and comfort. There's a *plonk* in the water—someone has plunged in.

"Tutu, go and find the stranger disturbing our peace this afternoon," Mama says.

She trusts me to be careful in my surreptitious movements.

"Mama, it's probably nothing serious," I reply, engrossed in applying mascara. "I am certain it's teenagers who can't do without their afternoon swim."

She believes in my judgment. If we are to survive here, we must lay low. Humans must not be killed. This is a rule sacrosanct to the tribes. The last thing we want is to draw fire from them. Rather than hurt them, we destroy their equipment—a strategy we learned from the merfolk.

There is another *plonk*. This time it shakes the peaceful waters. Imran calls my attention, says he sees a machine in the water. I lead the two teenagers in my company through the anfractuous boulders we built to conceal our presence. Living here has helped me glean information about the kind of human who comes to our shore. Besides the fishermen, teenagers skinny-dip, tourists smoke and toss their tiny cigarettes and scrunched cans into the water, and girls gossip seated on the sand, oblivious of me taking their make-up kits, no other humans have frequented the river until now.

"What do you think that thing is?" Imran asks, hiding behind a seamount jutting out of the wavy seaweeds.

"Oh no!" I say. "It's happening again."

"What's happening—" Olu cuts in.

I command him to remain silent. An aquanaut dives into the water. In his hand is a sonar device. We watch him gingerly work his way around a blue bathysphere. My best guess is they are just scientists who come to explore. Nothing more. A throbbing thought jumps out of my head: *Humans do not just explore the water, unless they take interest in it.* Imran suggests we scare him, give him the beating of his life. Olu is quick to remind him what will happen when the diver is out of the water telling his human-group about a bunch of selkies who attacked him. Olu is one of my bright learners; he has quickly understood the secrets of surviving in the deep.

The aquanaut completes his connections. As soon he leaves, I advance towards the bathysphere, scanning the wonders of human creation. *Eureka!* I mutter, when I find the main camera that would have allowed the intruders a complete view of our home, breaking it with a stone.

The council calls an emergency meeting. Amidst the fears being hurled around I try to find words of hope. The children are already clinging to their parents. The stories of what humans have done to our kind bring them a full course meal of nightmares. Even the plants shrink, recoiling at the mention of humans. I see mama's flippers quiver.

"No evil will come to us," I say, to allay the fears of their troubled hearts. "I will come up with a plan to drive them away. We will keep our new home safe."

They believe in me too much for me to fail them.

Later that night, when everyone is asleep, I creep out of my space, swimming all the way up. Slowly, I stick out my head, looking left and right to be certain no human is at shore. I know it's stupid, but my coming out here almost every night has become habitual. I strip off my coat, place it atop a scraggy rock rooted close to the shallow waters. Naked, I step from the waves and lie back on the sand. The feel of earth on my body is enchanting. Face up, I stare at the sparkling shy stars peeping from their cocoon: incongruously, the constellations form what appears to be a man, kneeling to propose to a selkie. This is a scene that plays in my head. Our kind are betrothed after birth. Ladi, the selkie I am betrothed to, is patient enough to wait for me till I am nineteen before we are joined in the ritual of selkie-man and wife. The waters climb on each other. At intervals, the foamy water touches my skin before retreating and joining the rest of its body. Humans are blessed creatures. I wonder why the ground they walk on is not enough to quench their pleasure. Perhaps they are solipsistic.

I am still basking in the tranquil breeze when a faint patter on sand contaminates my peace. I jolt up, scamper and hide close to a shack. A young man approaches, with dark-skin that beam in spotlight of the full moon. He stands akimbo, facing the water.

Around his neck is a strap clipped to a digital camera. He takes few shots, walking into the water, snapping the rock and the sky. From where I hide, I pray he doesn't find my coat. When he leaves, it's the cue for me to leave as well. I run to get my coat, don it with shaky hands, submerge deeper away from danger.

Back in bed I think of the human. Something about him is different.

Panic clouds the waters and carves unequivocal fright on everyone's faces the following morning. Black oil meanders atop the water surface, blocking the soothing warmth of the morning sun. No one knows what it is. But we fear such a substance will be toxic enough to kill us. Someone calls it black shit.

"The devilish humans will never know peace for invading our lands," another cries from the crowd.

Murmurations agitate the serenity. Mama holds me closer, scared that the curse has finally taken its grip on us.

"What do you suggest we do?" a council member questions.

All eyes are glued to me, waiting for a miracle answer. Dread crackles in my veins, whispering words of capitulation. Truthfully, I am void of an answer.

"You are the one who has spent the most time on the humans' land," another says.

"I can't tell you what that substance is," I reply, gulping some of the fear clogging my throat. "Humans will not stop driving us out of our homes. The only way out of this is to fight back. First, I will study them."

They all stare in befuddlement. Some of their mouths are ajar, trying to grapple with the gibberish I just uttered. How can I compare a selkie's strength with a human's? Their deadly weapons and war tactics? They will strike all of us down with a single barrage from their automated machine guns. The cowardice of the tribe's response irritates me—running away was always their way out.

I know the challenges facing me. My skin will desiccate if I linger on land for long after taking human form. Humans might discover my true identity, enslaving and interrogating me to give up the tribes' location. Human food could cause my stomach to swell, stiffen my innards, exploding from inside to cause an untimely death. But this is an inevitable mission, I think, and one that must be taken. Mama's teary eyes don't change my mind. Ladi's sweet words of conviction only brush the threshold of my consciousness.

I study the human for each of the four nights that he comes to take pictures. The black oil continues spreading across the water. The children are the first to experience wheezing. Something in the substance is baleful to their health. The time to act is now. The entry plan is this: Ladi will take custody of my coat and wait for me in the early hours of the morning where I will meet him to return to the deep.

"Be careful, my daughter," Mama says. "Humans possess dark hearts."

The oracle puts a unique shell pendant of intricate markings around my neck.

"The gods will keep you safe, child. Go in peace," he says, placing his adorned staff on my back while I genuflect in front of him.

I hand my coat to Ladi. He kisses me, wishing me luck on my quest. My heart beats irregularly when I think of this foolhardy mission. I can feel it attempting to force its way out of the cordoned barricade, separating itself from the other organs. I remain in the water, a scuba mask in my hand, with a bikini and lappa over my body—clothing I stole from careless humans.

I notice the human engage in his usual activity. He touches the black oil, rubbing it against his fingers.

"Help! Help!" I scream, acting theatrically as if trying to stay afloat.

He hears me scream and drops his camera, comes rushing into the water to save me. He pulls me out, lays me flat on the sand. Rushing words drop like pellets from his mouth.

"What is your name?" he ask with a charming tone.

Lounging in his aura, the chill and plush of his hands, I pretend that I'm unable to speak. His eyes remind me of the coral eyes of a merman I once fucked.

"Can you walk? Let's get you to safety," he says.

He loops his camera around his neck, helps me up, and slings my right hand over his shoulder. I look back, squinting, to find Ladi watching us. As the human takes me further, Ladi becomes blurry and distant. Soon I lose sight of him.

Sizzling sounds and a pungent smell kick me awake. What surrounds me isn't the feel of water on my skin, elodea beautifying the walls of my room, or a seahorse waking me up after I overslept. Around me are books hilled on a brown table, a kaleidoscope of rectangular pictures—both colored and black and white—of water and sea animals pinned on the wall. Wine bottles of various sizes are collected in a corner on a wooden stand, and a camera lies on a single cushioned chair. A tomahawk hung askew almost squeezes my heart with trepidation. There are other items I can't identify. My senses nudge me back to reality—I'm sitting on a bed with a cotton quilt, and wearing a shirt with the slanted, scribbled words, *I am married to the sea.*

This is happening. I am actually in a human's home. He appears, smiling, holding a tray of sweet-smelling food in his hand.

"I see you are finally awake," he says, placing the tray neatly on the bed.

I withdraw, staring into his eyes without speaking, maintaining a grim demeanor.

"My name is Koyo. You called out for help last night. What is your name? Where are you from?"

My attention is glued on the tray in front of me. Humans really know how to care for a guest. Koyo takes a bite, buttressing in action that his intention is not to poison me. I have seen this food before. The merfolk had a library before it was destroyed. Being an autodidact helped me garner all the needed knowledge. Koyo must paint me as a glutton after I devour the meal without civility. The hot tea scalds my tongue.

I spill out the cooked-up story for his perusal. *My name is Vivian. My family and I were on a boat cruise when we had an accident. I swam away from the fire as far as I could before you found me close to the shore.* The ploy works. He believes every word I say, assures me he will look for my family.

Dusk descends like a fog while I immerse myself in combing Koyo's room, flipping through his books, scanning everything that might give a direction on how to stop the pollution in our waters. I find nothing useful. At least nothing that indicates the reason for their inhumane acts.

Noises slither into my ear from outside. I grab Koyo's brown pants and go out to see for myself. The throng of humans engaging in their ceaseless talk spooks the living daylights out of me. *Blend in. Remain calm.* They ignore me, spitting rains of fury about how the government has given permission to foreigners to exploit the crude oil in their land. The exploration has led to the contamination of the lakes and rivers, destroying their staple means of livelihood. They too are beginning to suffer the same way we do. For the first time ever, I feel sympathy for them. Koyo is among the fuming villagers, airing out his grievances. I dodge him, making my way to the shack, waiting for Ladi to show up with my coat.

The tribe finds my words incredulous when I narrate the happenings on land. Some of them say I am growing a soft spot for the humans, defending their actions. Olu and the others are glad to see me, asking if the humans hurt me. Ladi's hug almost asphyxiates me. That night as I lie in bed, I bring out an orb which I stole from Koyo's room. Marooned in it is a small wooden ship having dummy sailors. I shake it, excited at the bubbles dancing about. Koyo clings to my mind. His hair, those enchanting eyes, pointed nose, the stubble. I have never known a fine human-man act with such benevolence before. I shove away thought of a blissful ending with him. Falling for him will place a grave curse on the tribe and bring ignominy to my family.

It is expedient that I return to the humans. Ladi frown against it, but he dare not counter the words of the oracle. The mission, our safety, our home is of utmost priority.

Koyo's mouth is ajar when he opens the door. I can't fathom if he is delighted to see me or vexed that I stole his orb and left without a word. He invites me in, asking where I've been. Succinctly, I tell of my adventure to the neighboring village, hoping to question anyone who might have seen my family.

"Why is this orb so important to you anyway," I say, when he requests I give it back.

"It's an heirloom," he says. "Come let me show you."

We walk past the walls of his room, covered in beautiful pictures. He speaks of his love for nature, particularly the sea. I ask about the tomahawk. He brings it down, places it in my hands. The weapon chills my veins. It was a gift from his grandfather. Having fed my eyes on so much, he sits me down. He bed pulls out a fusty box with inscribed images of whales and dolphins from under the bed.

"My late grandfather said he bought this box at a dockyard on his first trip to Zanzibar," he explains.

Contained in the box are sea shells of various colors still smelling of freshness, shot harpoons, a diary, miscellaneous water artifacts, and a photo album full of sepia colored images of his grandfather and other people. The eleventh page arouses abhorrence in me when I see seals caged in a trammel on top of a boat. As if to further ignite my ire, there are pictures of sealskin layered on the floor as men celebrate around this priceless material. It makes me cringe.

"Are you ok?" Koyo asks, noticing the scowl on my face.

I allow my anger to deliquesce, segueing to something else.

"I am starving."Do you have something I can eat?" I say, smiling sheepishly.

Koyo stands up, heading towards the kitchen to serve me a rechauffe. He inquires about my family. There isn't much to tell. He will call me demented if I reveal my identity to him.

"I saw some people gathered on the road the day I left," I say. "They seem furious."

"Their means of livelihood has been threatened. The government permitted an oil company to extract their crude oil, but the aftermath of this action is ruining our lands. Have you seen the water recently?"

It's apparent that we and humans are facing the same challenge. The question nudges me, chimes in my head—what can I do about it? We spend the rest of the day touring the village. Such peculiar monuments humans have. He buys me a swellegant flannel dress. We head to a local pub for a plate of pepper soup and palm wine. The palm-wine makes me a little dizzy. We listen to tales about the tradition of the land from grizzled old men.

Shit! I mutter.

It is difficult to escape from Koyo when all he does is stare and lace my fingers with his. Passing towards the beach that night on our way home, I know Ladi will be waiting with my coat. He quacks at me. Koyo hears it, too. I disentangle my fingers from him, allowing him to take pictures of me. *Click, click, click.* The shutter sound mixes with the whispering night breeze. I begin to remove my dress without shame, climbing out of it, walking to the beach.

"Someone might see you," Koyo says, looking back to be certain we are the only ones present. By the time he returns his gaze at me he has lost me. Beneath the rippled waters I tell Ladi of the mission, reminding him that I have to spend more time with the humans to gather enough information to report to the tribe. Annoyance clouds his face. He grabs my hand, forcing me to go down into the deep with him. I struggle, break free of his grasp, bobbing to the surface to the sight of a distressed Koyo.

"You scared me," Koyo says, panting. "I thought I had lost you again."

I rise, dawdle towards him, allowing him an undiluted stare at my naked body. He hands me my dress, we go home with my head on his shoulder. Days roll over days. Crude oil extends to the river and lake, slowly becoming a scourge. Humans can no longer go fishing. Koyo explains the adverse effect of this, how poverty and crime are the result of this unfortunate situation. I attend the community meetings with Koyo. The villagers agree that the foreigners responsible for this mess must pay for it.

I rest on Koyo after we pleasure each other, playing with the hair on his chest. Later, a sharp noise wakes us. We look from the window: a man carries a boy. A small hand dangles, lifeless. Sympathizers follow them, ululating intermittently. I watch the burial rites. The boy is buried near the riverbank, so that his soul can transcend to their afterlife without being a vagrant. Koyo rushes back home to get his camera. Every click brings bitterness to my heart, drowns me in a gloomy pool. *Pictures capture the emotions the heart cannot speak*, Koyo says. He is so engrossed in seizing these moments that for a minute I imagine he is oblivious to them.

When the sympathizers leave for their homes, Koyo simmers, ire erupting from him. A boy died today, most likely from swimming in the poisoned water. Who will be next? The tribe will suggest we take our leave once I mention this to them. We who inhabit the deep are prone to suffer. A final goodbye to Koyo is soon to come. A fisherman claimed to have found the boy's cold body on the wavy water surface. I know better than to think the child's death isn't cause by someone from my tribe. Patiently, I wait for the night to come.

Night. Koyo is snoring when I leave and shut the door carefully.

"I knew you would come," Ladi says, face caked with evil grins.

I look back at the stretched darkness draping the entire village, snatch my coat from him, plunging into the river. On our way home I ask if he had a hand in the child's death. His response is indifferent. It has to be him.

Mama is disappointed at my inconsiderate attitude, ranting about how I abandoned the tribe to spend time with the humans. The council commands I never see Koyo again. Other members of the tribe spare no time in expressing loathing towards my love for humans, saying I forgot my origins, reminding me why I was sent up there. I try to reason with them, emphasize the need to linger more with the humans, devise strategies to curb the pollutions ravaging our home. My opinions fall on deaf ears. The most important thing of all is protecting our home. For how long are we going to keep abandoning our homes once we feel threatened? This is the crux of my argument to the tribe. The oracle know my words to be true. After all, he breaks bread with the gods.

"I am pregnant by the human," I say, further aggravating their disgust.

Silence moves as an angry bird, flapping its wings. Mama falls backward. Deep in her eyes I see a volcanic steam of ire she had never shown before. Everyone avoids me, moves away from my presence. Olu pats me on the back as he leaves, an expression of disappointment on his face. The tribe has forgone the mission of protecting our home, they are getting ready to leave. As always.

Being ostracized from the tribe is an inevitable punishment for my act. At least I get to keep my coat and spend more time with Koyo. Sunlight angles in from the windows in his house, providing warmth on my feet. I'm curled up at one corner of the bed, thinking over my actions, wondering if Koyo is worth all of this. Then I hear it, the sound of feet trampling on the ground waking the sleeping dust. I peep and see some see people brandishing cutlasses, axes, and knives. My first thought is to go out and find Koyo. I am new in this settlement—where could I possibly go to look for him? I touch the shell pendant around my neck, praying to the gods for the bravery to face the hurdles on the road. Koyo rushes in and grabs his camera.

"Let's go," he says. "There's something you have to see."

When we get to the beach, my eyes fall on a sight my mouth couldn't express. The beach is thronged with both young and old. Part of the water is bloody. A sperm whale, presumably dead, lies in the water. Humans spare no time in cutting their chunks of meat from this helpless beast. The glee in their faces evokes rage in me. My guess is this meat will be a consolation for their days of not fishing since the black oil attacked their livelihood. Dead squids and few fishes fall out of the whale when a boy plunge his knife into its belly. The tribe must have been long gone. Koyo covers all of this with his camera. Sometimes I wonder if his penchant for pictures is a mere hobby, or if he wishes to keep them as a trophy rather than use them to help the villagers.

No single human in the beach shows a hint of remorse. Now I see the reason Mama doesn't like me mingling with them. The ones who have a basin full of whale flesh leave and others return, looking for a spot to cut their own share.

That night I spoke with Koyo, telling him how those people do not feel bad for their actions. I tell how I lost my family due to the environmental hazards of humans. I want to express a deluge of my revulsion for them. All of their actions from inception have been geared towards polluting the sea, lakes and rivers. Do they even consider the creatures living beneath? Perhaps they don't realize that their smug attitude would wreak great consequences on the sea dwellers.

Koyo is rapt. He has never found me to be a loquacious person. I admit I am a bit verbose.

"You sound like you are friends with a mermaid," he says, making a jest. "It's a good thing you mentioned it, I think I have gathered enough pictures to tell the world of what has been happening here. First, I need permission to post the picture of the dead boy," he says, with regret and hurt in his voice.

Dawn push away the stubborn darkness refusing to leave its space. We go to the late boy's mother, seeking her permission to share the burial pictures.

"Shey dis one go bring my pikin back," she ask, tears streaming down her face.

Koyo comfort her, assuring her that the pictures might be a first step in curtailing the actions of the company responsible for her misfortune. She gave him the go ahead. Koyo shares the pictures online, alongside the hashtags of various environmental bodies and news agencies, calling for the need to save the sea and everything that lives in and beside it. At intervals we check for the feedback on the pictures. The engagements are coming in.

After all that has happened, we think the gravest of disasters has already passed us by. We thought wrong. This is just the beginning. People start to fall sick. The majority of them are the consumers of the dead sperm whale. I need no soothsayer to tell me that the whale must have been poisoned by the black oil. The sea and river are no longer habitable for fishing and swimming. It has become a black murk of wastes and dead animals blocking the flow of sunlight and air into the deep. The tribe is right to have suggested we leave. I pray they are safe wherever they are.

I allow one of Koyo's neighbors to plait my hair when the sun is about setting, though part of its yellow ring is yet to leave the vast sky. Five people approach us. Their dress indicates they are not from around here.

"Hello," one of them says. "My name is Matilda. I was told I would find the photographer who took these pictures."

She holds out some of Koyo's pictures, printed in color. I still feel the remains of queasiness, seeing the skeletal frame of the dead whale.

"We are representatives of an international body protecting communities suffering from environmental hazards. We want to help bring an end to this menace," Matilda says.

I feel my body swathed in joy. Someone has come to our aid. They meet with Koyo, asking him to enlarge the pictures and pass them on while they take the necessary actions. The only thing the government did was temporarily close down the oil extraction project. The villagers know how it will all play out—once the heat of the moment is gone, the project will resume.

The moon appears as a crescent in the dotted sky. Koyo is fast asleep. I visit the river, bend under the red tape barricade used to restrict people from going beyond. It smells of putrid fish. I extend my walk into the stagnant water, pushing my feet through the obstacles of dead things. I sing to the river, its stench filling my body with disgust. We selkies communicate with our voices no matter how far away we are. Uncertain if my call will be acknowledged, I keep singing, stretching my voice far into the sullied air. My message is clear to the tribe; we are on the verge of victory, completely halting the project that has rendered the villagers jobless and made us lose our home. I wait for a reply from a member of the tribe, but their voices are silent.

Reporters of different television and radio stations set their equipment in front of the village square. The village had met, decided to march to the government house. In the hands of the village leader is an international signed petition demanding the government shut down further operations, demanding payment of damages, and demanding the guaranteed safety of the waters.

While reporters are questioning Koyo and the rest of the community, I sense I belong here with them. A huge part of me wishes the tribe was here. Then I feel a tap from behind: It's Olu, and he's smiling at me. Mama and the rest of the tribe are present, too.

"Ladi did a great deal of work in convincing us to come back. He reached out to the merfolks. I don't know what he did, but his words swayed them to come join in the march," Mama says. "He didn't kill the child. The child was already dead when he found him."

My distant relatives are prepared for this peaceful protest.

"Mama told me you deserve the praises for bringing the tribe here," I say to Ladi.

He shakes his head in disapproval.

"I simply gave them a reason to keep their faith strong. Ever since your ban I waited for your song. The night I heard it from the ripples of the water, I knew I had to do everything to support you.

Besides, I was tired of always having to find a new home."

I want to hear the words about his innocence of the dead child. I ask him.

"I took offence when you found love with the human. I wanted you to be as angry as I was. But I am no killer. The poor child died when he went swimming that night. The spillage must have made breathing difficult."

We file out en masse, holding placards and pictures. The humans sing in their native dialect, and the vigor in their voices cuts through the rising dusts and the levitating aura. We sing as well, in ours.

I am sunbathing in the beach when people point at a creature in the water. It's a seal, and the seal is Olu. People are taking pictures of him. Olu sees me, and calls to me before submerging into the deep. Fishing has not fully resumed. Our cries and demands yield results. The villagers received part-payment for the damages, and operations are permanently suspended. The water has not yet fully cleared, though we are hopeful that it will soon.

Koyo offered to help Olu get a job when I introduced him as my brother. But Olu's bond with the sea has not let him fully decide to start living on land.

"If I didn't know you well enough I'd say you share a common affinity with the sea," Koyo say, holding a necklace having a blue pendant he bought for me. I wear it around my neck, next to the shell pendant.

I giggle, shrug, and rub my protruding stomach. In few months I'll birth a child. Eventually I'll have to tell Koyo the truth. I hope that when I do, the affinities that we share will be enough.

Oyedotun Damilola is a Nigerian who writes contemporary and speculative fiction, and non-fiction about pop-culture.

His short story 'All We Have Left Is Ourselves' was one of the winners in the 2022 PEN America Dau Prize for Emerging Writers, and also the winner in the short story category in Android Press's First Annual Utopia Awards.

He has works published (and forthcoming) in *Reckoning*, *Kalahari Review*, *Omenana*, *Our Move Next*, *Solarpunk*, *Clarkesworld*, *Lightspeed*, Tor.com (*Africa Risen* Anthology), and *Science Fiction World*.

You can find him on Twitter: @dhamlex99

The Dream Catcher's Island

Ejiro Elizabeth Edward

Magic! That is the word I could use to describe where I came from, my island. It was not owned by any individual but a collective of small dwellers surrounded by bodies of water, a small place where I knew our neighbors' names, where I woke up to the serenity of the waves greeting me. I almost took this view for granted and lost my wonder of her.

I once lived close to the ocean, knew the smell of the ocean, I took care of the ocean in the ways of my people, and in turn she gave me life. Some days she would come bearing fruits of thanksgiving to my doorstep, foreign items I didn't know I needed until she brought them to me. The children of Tarkwa Island benefited the most from these gifts. When I was a new baby, my mother got from her a dream catcher she placed over my crib. My hands would stretch out to touch it, and as an adult I could remember the dream catcher hanging over my head, slipping into my dreams and drawing me into the water.

As a child, items from the ocean were used as toys, or sometimes our parents graced our bodies with them, like that one time I got a rainbow shell.

I still wear it on my neck.

But there were other days too, days she kissed the toes of the threshold of my house that barely stood together. She threatened to swallow us, but she did not. On days like this she gifted the community with even stranger things. Like the one time she vomited in front of our neighbor's house a lifeless human body. They said the body was round and swollen. I only heard about it; I was forbidden as a child to see those kinds of giftings from the ocean. But I grew up too and saw many gifts. I even saw the ocean give us the body of my childhood friend who had been missing for three days. I knew this loss, and it laced my tongue to remember that even when we were one with the water, the proverb remained: "*Being a swimmer and spending time in the water does not make you a fish*". We were surrounded by the ocean, and to survive the ocean we had to become like rocks.

You would think that I should be afraid of water. That it would come one day and swallow me into its mouth and just like that I would stop existing. But a land that inhabits you shouldn't be the one to kill you. I told this to outsiders who queried my bravery and rolled it on their tongue. Who came here to enjoy the water my island offered but ran back to the comfort of their homes when they grew tired of her beauty. Who would blame them? They had no idea how to pacify the water.

Children of the water returned back into the water. We were not like the outside world whose spirits roamed after death. When one of our own died, we would ship them into the middle of the sea and let them go back home. This was where they belonged, for the ocean held on to us, and if we didn't do that, that person's spirit would cry from beneath the grave, calling us to join them. We couldn't afford to let our community die, we knew the city world frowned on us when we did such things, but they had no say over our domain.

This was home. Home was ours.

The ocean was on an island, separated from the outside world. I watched the city people come and go. They came to our island to have a swell time, but for us this place was home, and home was threatened. Home was threatened by the city people, people who parked their cars at the edge of the city and took boats to our island to have some fun. They would come dressed in their fancy city clothes, wearing bourgeois sunglasses, for the sun our bodies adored. They came with food items, too tired to clean up after they left, making the environment uninhabitable for us. But we were gracious enough to pick up after them. There was already a system in place that allowed the men of our island to tax them so we could clean up the place. It was giving back what belongs to us, and they did.

During summer the children of the island, now men and ladies, showed off their talents. I, for one, blended into the ocean to show off my skills with my skateboard, synched with the wind, and in turn I got the admiration of the city people. I got job offers to teach these people, and I made respectable money for it. I didn't desire much—I was a wanderer, I needed only bread and fish for the soul.

Other times I saved people from our ocean. She was sometimes eager to eat those who didn't know how to flow into her rhythm, but she knew me well enough to be merciful.

I defended my island until I could no longer defend it. It was the year before covid-19 that the government came for us. The year 2018, when I woke up to ships and guns surrounding our small houses, with a loudspeaker waking me up from my dream saying: "*The government will be taking over this island, this island will now be used for military purposes*".

I imagined my ears to be filled with the sand from our island, that the seashells had covered them and that I was in a dream. The one where the sirens and the mermaids played tricks with my mind. Disbelief filled me til I thought I would drown in it.

Where would I go? Where was home if not here? I watched as the elders held countless meetings with government officials, days leading to months, til I began to shrug off the evacuation as nothing.

The island youths were angry. I was angry! Who would dare take our island from us? But I was powerless, and my tongue did the talking. Some of us, the youths who had access to social media, tweeted and trended for a week. I prayed that the city people would intervene. That they would save us. They did not.

It was decided that we would evacuate the premises, but we would be compensated. But how much could compensate for home, for her? For the smell of water? To wake up to the ocean and dive into her. To have your body know the waves. To become one with her. To have access to her. Our evacuation was due next year, but I was already swollen with sadness.

My eyes filled, and the tears dropped into the ocean.

In those days, the ocean was quiet. It was peaceful, it followed us in mourning, it could sense our loss, collective loss.

The island was slowly being cleared by the government with the installation of small camps. I watched as the elders of our island sold off our homes for five shillings, like Judas selling off Jesus to his cross. The betrayal burnt the bones of the youth in Tarkwa Bay. Where would we go and call home? Some heard this news with great joy, receiving a call to swap their consciences for a desire to leave.

Eventually, people started leaving, but my foot was rooted here. The bodies of my mother and siblings were buried deep in the ocean. How would I carry their presence into the busy city? Into a land where vehicles smothered the skin of humans in exhaust. Where their water rushed through pipes into their homes, while all I had to do was drink from the ocean.

I wasn't ready. A few of us stayed back to defend our home, until the men with machine guns came at night and bullets dropped like rain onto our houses and we fled. Four years later, the world has moved forward and the city people have more access to our island, but this time the government is in control.

The city isn't for people like me. I have watched my body shed skin to adapt to this new environment. It still doesn't fit my webbed feet which are used to carrying the weight of sand. Not this concrete ground and cemented rooftops that threaten to take the air out of my lungs. This city where the clouds swallow the stars and hide them. It's been years, and my body still can't adapt to this environment. They say that man evolves, but all I wanted to evolve into was the sea.

As a child, I played mermaid with my island friends. Now my people are scattered all over this city, trying to blend in and become a part of it. But an ocean child is forever an ocean child, and when this city finally sleeps, I will return to her.

Ejiro Elizabeth Edward is a female artist from Nigeria. She is the winner of Antoa poetry contest 2021. She has been published in *HOAX*, *down river road*, *Native Skin*, *Consequences Forum*, *Lolwe*, *Serotonin*, and *Isele*, amongst others. She is the convener of Benin Arts and Book Festival. She looks forward to being an MFA student. Find her on Twitter: @Ejiroedward552.

LITTLE APOCALYPSES

Aparna Paul

one.

Fall is the season of memory, or so my mother always told me. Every leaf turns in its delicate dance with death. They beckon us to recall what the world looked like flush with green newness, what it looks like revealing grey emptiness. My mother was scared of the winter, of an infinite dark sky, ashes falling from the clouds.

In the fall, she would instead ask me to remember. Every autumnal equinox, she walked into my room and fed me a fairy tale, something warm to press back against the cold and dark of the night. It would begin like this:

"This is a story about the end of the world."

And it always was. When I was six, this was the equinox story she told me:

"This is a story about the end of the world. There's a fault line that runs the length of a state, through the middle of a city. And one day, but I don't know when, it's going to split it all down the center. This is a city with buildings that reach to the sky like trembling fingers, and buses crawling its streets like beetles in the garden, and a *liveliness*, a pulse of history. It's always raining in the city, I think, and no one dares look towards the precipitous heavens."

She took my hand then, and I almost lost the thread of the story, distracted by the way her fingernail curved around the tip of her middle finger, hugging close to the dry skin there.

"One day, this fault line shivers. Everyone is looking at the ground, they see the way it ripples below their feet. They look up then, in fear. They look at the person on the sidewalk next to them, at the table to their right, across the aisle on the bus. Their mouths are pressed closed, but their eyes have changed. Their eyes are open now. 'Did you feel that?' their eyes ask. Not 'did you *see* the way the ground shook.' Not 'did you *hear* the way the earth groaned.'

Did you feel that? Did you feel it, same as I, the way the world felt it too? Did you feel it like a rumbling sadness, or a shaking anger, or something a little like love?

"You know the rest, I'm sure. The world split open like an egg. The streets ripped themselves apart. The cars all fell into the abyss, and the buildings, and the cobblestones, and the sewer grates, and the fire hydrants, and the everything, the all of it, the things that they built and called indestructible. When it was all done falling into the chasm, even some people, I think, the remaining few looked at each other, *really looked*, and they said, *did you feel it, too? Do you know where we go next?* And even if they couldn't answer the question then, they gazed back at each other, and they tried to find an answer in the ruins.

"That's how the world ends, tonight," she whispered, and kissed me on the forehead. She turned out the lamp, and stood in my doorway, a silhouette against the light in the hall. She looked over her shoulder in a promise to me—to our home—that she would return, as if she would be gone a long time. The next morning, of course, she opened the door and gently shook me out of the little apocalypses in my dreams.

two.

In the fall of my seventeenth year, the skies greyed and the leaves turned with an urgency I'd never seen before. The world was dry as a bone, the sweet summer humidity sucked away as cleanly as marrow. Life felt empty, empty, empty, but when I stumbled home on the equinox, I was full, so full, of light and laughter and warmth. A little too much liquor. A rose would envy the blooms of my cheeks.

I pressed open the door, ever so quiet, and there she was on the couch. Wrapped in a blanket, gaze fixed on the wall. I was swaying in my too-tall black boots, trying to remember what day it was, when she turned to me, holding out a glass of water. She made me take off my shoes, walked me up the stairs.

She was all sighs and tired eyes, and I didn't know it then, but there was nothing like disapproval there. There was only joy and reassurance in her heart, even if it didn't know how to make itself known.

I sat on the bed, toed off my socks, my shoulders readying to flinch against her reprimand. But instead: "This story is about the end of the world," she said. I tried to stop her, thinking of the personal statements and exam scores and recommendation letters on the hard drive of the downstairs computer.

I don't need any other stories, I thought. *I know my own, and I know how I've written it. I know how the rest of the words will write themselves*—"And I don't need to hear the stories you're going to say." She looked at me, then, her eyes dark and sorrowed and liquid, and she refused to stop.

"This story is about the end of the world. It started with the birds. They took to the skies, a streak across the blue, a cloud, if a cloud could be angry. Then the deer, crossing the road in front of cars. They were already limping, great lacerations in their haunches, fear in their eyes. And all the people in the town, they only noticed the intricacy of the antlers, not the way that they stared.

"The world was trying to share the most difficult truth in the universe: its heart was broken. When our hearts are broken, we feel like we only know brokenness. Everything that we touch, we think, breaks too. That is the greatest tragedy, that we blind ourselves to reality. Nothing is broken because we have touched it. It is *transformed*. It is made anew. The world, too, wants to transform, wants to make anew. The world is dry, and searing, and wounded. From there, it's only a small step to wildfire. The blaze sweeps over our little lives, and its heart, its heart, wants nothing more than to feel warm, to share its warmth, to *transform* and make anew the coldness that is locked away in each of us. It does make something new, but this story isn't about that. It's about the end of the world, the ashes and the smoke and a hand pushing out of the scorched earth and into the steaming air, always, always reaching for the light, and reaching for each other."

She stood, paused at the door, looked back. "Good night," she whispered, but I was already falling, the alcohol dulling and dizzying the room. When the lightning bolt moon woke me up before the dawn, I'd already forgotten that she sat on the bed, that she told me a story. The blankets were disarrayed, and there was no impression of her in the mattress.

three.

When I was 27, there was no moon on the equinox. Nothing but silent dark. Earlier, I had stormed into my apartment, my roommate startling at the timbre of my footsteps. "Are you okay?" she asked, the paused TV a glossy reflection on her wide eyes.

"Yeah," I said, leaning against the counter. "My mom and I got into an argument."

"About what?"

"I don't know. What mothers and daughters always fight about, I guess. How to survive." She blinked at me, inviting more explanation, but I had nothing left to give.

Instead, I laid in bed under the moonless sky, looking out at the streetlamp across the road, its brilliant orange Cyclops eye a beacon in the misty dark. *What does the light illuminate, and what does it leave in the dark?* My mother, in a fluorescent-bright kitchen, all the light in the world, and the shadows spiraling from the man across the scarred wooden table. My voice, inherited from the greatest storyteller I knew. In each exaltation and whisper and pause, in each valley and peak, she was there. All those cadences, and I couldn't convince her to leave.

Apocalypses abound. The end of the world is unnervingly quiet, static on a telephone wire. Light slanted across my curious eyes, even as they closed, even as I slipped away.

In the morning, a voicemail: "This story is about the end of the world. This time, it happens in a city on a coast, where the ocean hugs the land. The ocean loves too much, if there were such a thing. It loves the timid ground and the blazing skies, but most of all, it loves the moon. But this isn't a story about the ocean, or the moon, or love. It's a story about the winter, which threatens to freeze the waters and the people and the everything into something static and immovable. Before all that, though, in this city on the coast, life is good. It's a city that you can always find a parking spot in. A city that has the best sandwich in the whole world right around the corner. A city that makes your legs ache because you never want to stop walking it. Who lives here? Let me tell you. People who have forgotten what love is, almost. Every night, they look out at the ocean, and they see the way that it crashes on the shore, and it reaches for the moon, and they wonder what it feels like to yearn and to want and to love.

"Until one night, the ocean rises, the wind stirs it into hurricane, and the waters crash against the buildings, they swallow until there's nothing left, nothing but an *I wonder why the ocean moves just so* echoing in the empty air. Good night, my love."

four.

A decade later, I picked up the phone when my mother called. She was living with my estranged brother; we were connected by a straight line interstate, with an impossible ocean of time and space stretching between us. I couldn't remember what the backs of her hands looked like. When her voice crackled out of the faraway silence, her words were laced with a distress I only heard when she talked about the winter. "Get me out of here," she said, and it was the only time in my whole life that she had ever called me and told me, exactly, in no uncertain terms, what she wanted.

I crossed two state borders that evening, helped her pack, noticed how the dry skin around her middle finger was peeling even worse than it was twelve years ago, how the fingernail on her left thumb was ridged and distressed. I remembered more than I thought I did. I packed faster, hands folding and compressing and pushing down, the only place I knew how to direct my force.

In the car, speeding against the twilight, we were quiet, only the steady hum of the fan between us. The road stretched out, languid and lazy beyond the windshield. There were too many cars on the highway for an arbitrary Tuesday twilight, and my shoulders were hunched, fingers tight.

A car swerved into the lane ahead of us, close, close, close, like the metal was aching to be touched, even if it meant being destroyed, and I pressed against the brakes with too much force.

The silence between us was tense, after, and I said, "I'm sorry." She looked at me, and I could feel her eyes on me, in the weighted way that mothers look at daughters, with hope and love and fear. "I know," she said. A pause. "This is a story about the end of the world."

five.

At thirty-eight, on the equinox, I don't understand what she's saying. Her eyes are as clear and bright as always, but her traitorous tongue speaks words beyond my scope. A language I never learned. The soft rhythms and smooth vowels of her childhood, narratives beyond my grasp, a brief word here or there, but nothing like a story.

And as my confusion grows, her panic becomes more pronounced. Quivering words and shaking hands and a crease between her brows. She takes my fingers in her own, wraps them tightly, tries to press the words between our skin since the air was so inadequate. I hold onto her.

I say:

"This is a story about the end of the world. Imagine a mother and a daughter. Imagine two women, with the darkness of a whole universe pressing against them. Imagine the light between them, the thing that keeps them awake, and alive. The thing that puts them to sleep, without any fear at all.

"Can you picture this? But how is this the end of the world, you wonder? How is this anything except beautiful? It's the end of the world, you see, because that galaxy between them is gone. The thing that they created together, the landscapes and the oceans and the valleys and the hills and the jungles and the deserts and the trenches and the caves, it's not there anymore. The world ended. Questions, questions, questions, and not an answer to be found. Fall is the season of memory. Every equinox, you asked me to remember. And I do, I finally do."

When she closes her eyes, the world ends.

Aparna Paul (she/her) is a writer, banana bread enthusiast, chemical engineer, and amateur crossword constructor. She is a regular performer and sometimes host at the Boston Poetry Slam. Her work has been recognized by *Gordon Square Review* and *LED*, and she edited and published an anthology with Literary Cleveland entitled *Reflections of The Land: Meditations on Environment & Industry*. When not writing, she's most likely playing cards or calling to a stranger on the street and saying "Look! The moon!"

Sacral

Amanda Yskamp

Amanda Yskamp's work has appeared in such magazines as *Threepenny Review*, *Hayden Review*, *caketrain*, *Redivider*, and *The Georgia Review*. She lives on the 10-year flood plain of the Russian River. She teaches writing from her online schoolhouse and serves as librarian at the local elementary school.

Ocean Vengeance

Maria S. Picone

She drowned & kept
drowning, surrounded by water
like her country
submerged until neither
ghost nor body rose; she became
a foaming of wave,
a froth of tide,
an erased border—

coming in for those who made
war & marked
graves like hers, who made
missiles & marked
targets like her, who made
ships & murdered friends of hers,
corporate bureaucrats stuffed
with sea stolen profits
in the neon city.

She streamed like a signal
through the network of yeoks—
samusil pipes froze & burst;
corrupt men slipped on winking ice;
coastal playhomes went under same
as her. The wicked turned fretful
eyes like dirty coals to sinks & gutters.

Water maidens coming for the Earth, they said.
Gwisin coming back to claim the sea.

From elderly ajummas in basement hovels
she took the water
mildewing cherished photos, moldering rice.
To canvassers signing up folks

to save the planet, she coalesced
another sip in reusable bottles.
A lost traveler at a mountain stream
swore he saw her, in a school uniform,
pointing the way back home, she,
mercy & wrath in tidal force,
surging—

Maria S. Picone/수영 is a queer Korean American adoptee. She won the 2020 Cream City Review Summer Poetry Prize. She has been published in *Tahoma Literary Review*, *The Seventh Wave*, and *Best Small Fictions 2021*. She has received support from The Juniper Institute, *Kenyon Review*, and *Tin House*. She is *Chestnut Review*'s managing editor, a SFWA associate member and an SFPA member. Find out more at mariaspicone.com, Twitter @mspicone.

Inclement Weather

Susan L. Lin

Paved roadways run across my body like a complex system of exposed veins and arteries. Over the years, they've carried you from one milestone in life to the next.

By bus or by car.

On bike or on foot.

But our relationship, as it currently stands, is unsustainable. None of this will last forever.

1994: The first time you ever saw snow. Microscopic flakes fell from the sky and melted as soon as they touched your tongue. They melted as soon as they touched me, too.

There's no way to sugarcoat the truth of what I'm about to say.

I'm drowning. That writing has been on the wall for decades.

You already know. You've been watching, wide-eyed, since you were a small child.

1997: A rare ice storm left all of us shivering. School canceled for the day, your parents' raised voices shaking frozen water from the tree branches outside. By then, you were used to their shouting matches. But that night, you heard glass shattering for the first time. The model ship your uncle once constructed was no longer safe inside its bottle-home.

When the water finally claims every surface of my body, inch by rising inch, I'll sink further below sea level.

Meanwhile, the ones who remain will slowly adapt the only way they know how.

1999: Your mother drove you to your new school in a Chrysler minivan so old it had racked up more miles than you ever will. She was behind on car payments and your father's last child support check bounced, but you knew you weren't supposed to know about that. You also knew that when the two of them fled their homeland after the Vietnam War, this wasn't exactly the sanctuary they'd been hoping for. In the hallways between classes, everyone joked the world would end on New Year's Eve. You secretly hoped they were right.

It may take time for evolution to do its thing.

You won't even notice the changes at first.

But then, as the overflowing bayou envelops you, you'll realize you're more than prepared to ride the waves.

2001: The world didn't end, but middle school did. One week later, the flood Allison left in her wake pulled me under for days. You watched the water creep up to the doorstep, the taste of calamity on your lips.

Survival mode will kick in. Probably sooner than you think.

One day, you'll discover in amazement that you've begun taking on boat-like properties: You have rudders where your ears once were. Your arms are beginning to look suspiciously like oars.

2005: You moved an hour away after graduation, the equivalent of leaving my kneecap for my ribcage. What came next? An Ivy League university. The cheerleading squad. A white boyfriend who bought you beautiful jewelry and always made you laugh. Everything the media had conditioned you to want since you were born. But even then, new storms kept coming ashore.

You'll adapt, you realize. You'll evolve. Maybe you'll sprout sails that billow in the wind like a pair of wings. You've always wished you could fly.

But you're all fools if you think any of this is a viable solution.

2011: I was parched for most of that summer, my normally dewy epidermis brittle and flaky. You went west in search of a graduate degree while fires blazed all around us.

In the future, if you return to visit me, you'll think how wonderful it must feel to be a submarine. After all, they can still get close to all the familiar landmarks you remember from your childhood.

Look, there's the state park where you used to hike with your dad, back when you still spoke to him! And isn't that the pizza parlor you used to frequent with your friends after your parents' ugly divorce? Oh, and let's not forget the mall where you were window shopping when you found out you got a full ride to one of the top universities in the country.

It will all be underwater by then, of course, and none of the boats on the surface will see what's lurking beneath.

2017: Harvey knocked, then forced his way in when I wouldn't open the door. That was the first time I thought the future might be arriving even more quickly than advertised. You watched in horror from the West Coast, where the weather was bone-dry. Where, in mere seconds, wildfires ate away at trees my brothers and sisters spent years cultivating. And that white boyfriend, the one you married, the one who made you laugh? It turns out he made you cry, too.

The future doesn't have to be this way.

Our final forms aren't set in stone. The window is shrinking, but there's still time to carve out a different tomorrow.

2021: Uri arrived in middle of a global pandemic. My skin no longer glowed. My body literally freezing. So many left powerless. The only accessory your ex gave you that you still wore was a silk ribbon wrap bracelet threaded through an anchor charm, the word *unsinkable* stamped on the aluminum. It was on your wrist when you finally made contact with your mother two thousand miles away, crying tears of joy with the knowledge that you were both still alive on this planet together, at least for another day.

Susan L. Lin is a Taiwanese American storyteller who hails from southeast Texas and holds an MFA in Writing from California College of the Arts. Her novella *Goodbye to the Ocean* won the 2022 Etchings Press novella prize and is now available to purchase at https://susanllin.wordpress.com/, where you can also find more of her published work.

P-T

Micah Nemerever

there will never be so many sea lilies.

they will never roll like meadows and lace
their brittle eyelash hands, nod
their heads and kiss. their endless

fields will smother
on ash. they will bow their necks
and break, the ending world

will fall on them like snow

soft shards of dead things.

one day you will lift
your withered hand and touch
the coffee cup to your paper lips,
and it will shatter at your feet
and that's

all. there will never be so many
of your eyelashes, or the stars.

one day you will kiss your dog's
forehead and leave him with a friend, walk
into the woods and never
come out.

one day the sea
will burn, and life will choke
again. buried corpses curdled black
into the slow revenge of
the Siberian Traps. you will hear on the news
everything you knew but
couldn't stop.

the tanks will roll in.
they will bring the villagers
past the barbed wire to see what
was done in their name, and some will cry
some will even mean it

one day you
will

until then, the asphalt
buckles with dandelions. until that day
you will walk the dog, and brush your teeth

and a fungus that eats radiation will grow in
Chernobyl.

until you die, and after
there will be your fingerprints

scrawled on the palms
of beautiful creatures, loved ones
who will also die,
and what you leave behind

will matter, spread like fields
of chipped exoskeletons
across the sea floor,
because to

matter
and to last forever
are not the same. after you

and after the white rhinoceros, after the
ash kills the lilies and blacks the sky, after
nearly all the sea
is snow

there will be the lilac tree
until there isn't, and there will be

another fungus, soft saffron-yellow folds
devouring its roots. there will be

little scrambling creatures who rush
into the absences, and after you
they will drink the carbon air

and flourish somehow even where
you couldn't.

after you and
everyone,
there will even

be sea lilies

not so many as before

but enough.

"P-T" originally appeared in *SLICE* #26.

Micah Nemerever was trained as an art historian. He wrote his master's thesis on queer identity and gender anxiety in the art of the Weimar Republic. His debut novel, *These Violent Delights*, published with Harper Books in 2020. His poetry and fiction can be found in *SLICE Magazine*, *The Carolina Quarterly*, and elsewhere. He lives in the Pacific Northwest.

What It Means to Love a City

Morris Hinkle

"How often does it happen, lad? You'll never see another in your lifetime."

The driver of the cart had not stopped talking since he'd found the boy, hot and alone, on the side of the road. The boy had the impression that he had never actually started talking, that he had been born with words tumbling out of his mouth and evaporating into the desert air.

"Once in a lifetime, that's what this is. Lucky to see it. Lucky to live it. And what a business opportunity! Lucky, lucky. Born at the right time, you and me."

The boy tucked his head over his knees and watched the road appear behind them in lurches. It was a new road, only as old as the city itself, but the sand had already been pressed darker than the dunes shifting all around them.

He had a lot of time to study the road. They moved when the cart before them did. They stopped when the cart before them stopped. The sun beat down and made the ground shimmer and crack.

It was cool enough under the cart's canopy. The driver sat with his feet up, ankles crossed over his front bar. He busied himself eating a fresh fruit, his hand held under his scarf to protect the intimacy of his lips. The boy could hear him slurping at the liquid spilling from the ripe flesh. A spill of words. A slurp of nectar. Repeated again and again.

"You can see the shape of it now, clear as day." *Slurp.* "Damn, it's a young one! I've never seen a city this young before." *Slurp.* "What a face. Don't you want to look?"

The boy tucked his marked hand between his knees and watched the road.

It was sunset by the time they drew close to the city. Guards grew from dots of holy red to fully articulated figures, armed and serious. Flashes of orange sparked as the papers they examined caught and reflected the dying sun.

"It's business approval for me," the driver told the boy. "Paid a pretty penny to make sure these were all in order. No, we won't have any trouble getting through with these." His voice was pink and misty with confidence. "Well, I won't at least. Better get yours out, son." He spent the next few moments shuffling, rearranging, checking. His papers pulled off each other with a drier version of the noise his mouth had made over the fruit.

"Can't get into a city as fresh as this one without good papers." *Strp.* "They don't let in just anyone, you know!" *Lick, strp.* Then, as they got closer to the guards and the boy still did not move—"You do have papers, don't you?"

The guards took their time checking over the driver's stack. "Business papers are often forged," they explained. "Anything to get into the city." The scavenging animals circled on the hot drafts overhead.

The driver pulled up his scarf so they could check his likeness against the one he carried. "Sorry, so sorry for the impropriety. You understand."

"Yes, yes. A city as young as this . . . ."

"What about you, lad?" The guard that asked leaned down to do it. His voice was kind, if tired. He wore an anatomical heart pendant around his neck. There was a black mark on the back of his left hand.

"I picked him up on the roadside," the driver was quick to say. "I don't know him."

The boy revealed his face, offering up a single paper. The guard frowned at the lonely sheet, confused. Then he let out a little gasp. He showed it to the other guard, who began to stare at the boy.

The boy hunched further over his knees.

"It is an honor," the guard with the pendant said as he handed back the paper. He did not hide the way he stared. The boy pulled his cloth up quickly, trying not to meet the guard's eyes. "May I be the first to welcome you to this great city."

"Thank you," the second guard said, "to you and your family." The boy could hear it in his voice: sorry, so sorry for the impropriety. The back of his left hand was unmarked.

"What's this?" the driver asked. "What's this?" But no one was paying attention to him anymore.

The boy had never been in a city before. Or, rather, he had never been in a city that still lived. He'd had the privilege of living in bones, in a place where the nutrients of a dying city had soaked into the eternal desert and created a rare oasis. He had looked up and seen stars framed in ribs, not endless walls of flesh. His feet had touched grass and sand, not tile and bone. He'd worried about burning his own skin and had never considered the impact of the sun on another.

As a child, he had been fascinated by the idea of the living cities. In school they had been presented as the height of civilization—of technology, of magic, of societal sacrifice. They were what made it possible for humanity to exist.

"Propaganda," his father told him. "To make people feel better about having to live in those places." His parents had been wealthy—not so wealthy that they had lived in the green, but wealthy enough that he had grown up knowing what green was, rather than only red and white and whatever color the sand took as the sun flashed against it and blinded you.

"It's gauche," his mother would agree. "Living caged in flesh. Can you imagine it?"

"The damn government is all over you in those places. You can't do this, you have to do that. Regulations, regulations, regulations. No, trust me. You're lucky to see the sky."

Still, he had been curious. He and his brother had poured over illustrated books page by page, late into the night, their marked hands crossing over each other as they shared the joy of discovering what else might exist outside of their comfortable home. Under cover of darkness, they had promised each other that, one day, they would see those cities in person.

He was finally here. The boy pulled his hood further over his eyes and fought the urge to vomit.

"Where do you want to go?" They were the first words the driver had spoken since the checkpoint. "Really, it's no problem. I'm happy to take you wherever you want. The Heart, I'm sure. I'd have to hitch the beasts, but if anyone has a right to skip the lines, it would be—"

"Where are you going?" the boy interrupted.

"I was headed to market. But I'm not sure that you'd.... I mean, it's not very...." The driver trailed off.

There had been markets in the book, filled with still people that shone with gloss as the pages turned. The idea of it had always bored him. What was exciting about a market? There were technological marvels to behold; there were sutures and ribs that divided and returned and the extraction of bones to make homes. Why would he want to look at people when he could look at the way they had learned to take a body and turn it into infrastructure?

Bile rose in his throat. He had to choke it down before he could respond. "I think," he said, almost as if he were in a dream, "that the market would be best."

The market smelled like iron.

"You sure you don't want to go to the Heart?" the driver asked. Again.

"Thank you," the boy told him, "for the ride." He held out a small coin.

The driver pulled away, slipping his hands into his pockets and pulling them behind his back. "Oh, no," he explained. "I really can't accept that. It wasn't any trouble."

As children, the boy and his brother had often played this game. "Oh, no, it was an honor." "No, the honor was mine," they would trade, one with hands in pockets behind his back, one with a coin that must be placed in those pockets. It was a dance they mimicked from court proceedings and the dinners their father hosted and attended, one they unconsciously rehearsed so they could take part in it when it mattered.

It mattered now. The boy did not take part. He placed the token on the seat of the cart, turned, and walked away.

There were many, many people in the market. The boy was sure there would be many, many more once the long line out in the desert was sorted through, once permanent vendors found and fought for and won their favorite spots and the loyalty of their customers, once the market visas for visiting shops were allotted. The ministers had been happy to talk about the vibrant commerce of a city, and he had been happy to listen. It was the only part he could follow. It was the only thing that still made sense.

Still, it was one thing to hear a minister say there would be a market and another thing to watch the vendors set up their stalls. The air was thick and strangely wet. Voices caught rather than carried as if even they weren't sure of their direction in this new city.

An argument caught his ear. He turned towards it without thinking, drawn by the way the sharp conversation cut through the air.

"—my last city," the man was saying. He looked glum. A drill hung limply in his hand, looking heavier than it had any right to be. "No one complained about it there."

A small woman stood before him. It was her fury that hung heavy on his drill. "This one is young." She enunciated every word as if she were speaking to a child. "You'll hinder his growth. You'll hurt him."

"It's just a shell. Meat and bones. It's not like it's alive."

The small woman snatched the drill from his hands. "I'll see to it that you lose your license for that."

"Try it. Take it up in the Heart itself if you have the money or the balls. Better yet, why don't you—"

A crowd began to gather. The boy moved on.

If the boy had looked up, he would have seen sinew, and muscle, and the honored stitchwork that was needed to hold these things together. He would have seen layers upon layers of homes, then businesses, then homes again, as neighborhoods took shape within the framework of the city's body. He would have seen the engineers hanging from scaffolding, could have watched them rework the bone and blood until they sustained not only the city body but the city occupants as well.

He did not look up. It was enough—almost too much—to smell the iron in the air, and to feel the way the ground gave way slightly under his feet.

Stepping directly on the city was supposed to be a crime. There were many things that were supposed to be crimes. He had them listed in a small book in his breast pocket, bound in red.

The half-built market only had a small tile path. It was clear that it was meant to act as a temporary footpath until they could build the beautiful, lasting streets that would come. It was also clear that whoever had thought a path a few tiles wide would suffice had never been to a market. Men, burdened and blinded by stacks of product, commandeered the whole track or forwent it completely. Others crisscrossed the open spaces as they built stalls and dismantled carts, porting supplies and instructions to the others who built stalls and dismantled carts. Every time the boy was forced to step off the path onto the soft, forgiving surface of the city itself, he felt as if he might cry.

He caught, suddenly, the smell of meat pies in the thick of the iron and wet. In this overwhelming newness, the familiar scent made him dizzy with nostalgia. He found the shop quickly. It was the only one with smoke churning from its chimney. That was against the rules, too. No chimneys except for the holy kilns. The priests were supposed to enforce this strictly, to maintain air quality and protect the precious lungs. Two priests were leaving the shop, chatting happily as they snacked on fresh pies.

He ducked under the cloth to find a warm space overfull with the smell of pies and the words falling from the shopkeeper's mouth. She gave a quick nod to the boy, but her attention was on a man cracking open boxes and unloading the contents in the corner. He stood pressed against the wall, trying to find space for leverage in all the clutter.

"—expect me to respect a clean-handed inspector. There are only two types of people who have clean hands. The rich and the ones who think they should be rich. Then again, there are only two types who enter the pool. How many, kid?"

The boy held up two fingers.

"The devout and the desperate." She shook her head as she popped two steaming pies into a bag. Her large heart pendant swung in time with her movements. "This one is devout. You can tell his family wasn't starved, can't you?"

The man unloading boxes tried to wave her words away, his face pinched.

"What? Am I wrong? I don't know what they were thinking, choosing a kid with this much fat." She handed the pies to the boy. "Two, huh? Bought one for a lucky girl?"

The boy paid for the pies and ducked out of the door.

His father used to buy them pies. His mother never did. "Not that greasy food again," she'd complain when he brought them home. "It's bad for the children."

"It's a good thing I bought these all for myself, then," his father would rib. He would split the pie bag at its seams, spreading it out like a tablecloth. The boys would sit, giggling, giddy with expectation, as they watched him lay the pies out like fine dining. He always made such a show of arranging them as if it were a table for one. "Since no one else wants any."

Their mother would come to the table, taking a pie from the pile with a huff and look of disdain and then she would proceed to eat more than anybody else. Those were the best days, pie days. They could even get his mother to laugh, sometimes.

His father also used to buy them gifts. Every year when the tax breaks went into effect and the pool bonuses came, so too came a pile of presents for the boy and his brother. They had loved that part of the year.

His mother had not. "They're not one of your investments!" he'd heard her shout once. He'd been carefully supervising his brother as he played with the brand new horse their father had bought them. It was made out of beautifully painted wood and every joint could be moved independently.

"You two have made me good money this year," he'd told them, laughing, as they unwrapped the gift. They would tell that to the other boys in school when they bragged about their new toys. We make our father good money. You should enter the pool. The chances of being chosen are so slight, and the tax breaks so great. Things their father had said around them. Things they repeated to each other as they lay on their stomachs and stared at the wonderful images of those civilized, living cities.

The new path the engineers had laid dumped him onto what seemed to be a main street, so he took that. Then he found a small set of stairs that led up and so up he went, first to a platform, then to another, until he was high enough to look down and see the busy mass that was the blossoming market. He clutched the warm bag in his hands. He imagined the grease on his tongue, in his stomach. He had to close his eyes and breathe for a long time before he could continue to climb.

The air around him shuddered noticeably here. If he looked to his left he could have peered through the ribs to see the lungs, working to pump oxygen to the living flesh that kept the ever burning sun at bay. If he looked to the right, he would see that flesh at work, close enough to touch.

He looked at his feet. The stairs were brown tile. The platforms were slightly lighter brown tile. He continued to climb.

He heard the next platform before he saw it. First it was a hum of voices, trickling down the tile steps. Then it became a cascade, the structure shaking with the force of hundreds of feet moving at once.

The steps widened, spilling the boy out onto a platform filled with ornate tiles organized into intricate patterns. He stood in the entranceway, frozen by the sudden pour of noise and population. Throngs of city dwellers, some still in their desert cloaks, most in city clothes more suited to the dark and damp, milled about with a restless intention.

"—long to install the lifts," he heard a man complain as he passed by. "I know it's good to thank him, but these damn stairs—"

An energetic child bounced along the path, vibrant offerings in his marked hands. The child was right about the age where he could be chosen to be a city himself. His mother held the back of his shirt tight, knuckles white. The look in her eyes was so protective, so relieved, that the boy turned away.

Dark red robes were common here, so close to the Heart. This was the realm of the venerated engineers and architects who made a body into a city, a city into a home. A group of them passed so close to the boy he could smell the incense clinging to their robes.

"—from the sternum," one finished.

"I'm worried about integrity," said another. "The regrowth—"

The intricacies of the city structure were one of the things he had not asked the ministers. They had been hesitant to tell him. He had been hesitant to ask.

"—split that one into two, and then take—" he heard.

"—too hard, I've gone through three saws—" he heard.

"—peel the top layer off, and then get to scraping—" he heard.

He stopped listening. He pressed his veil to his face and kept his eyes on the way the tiles seemed to float in space.

A woman found him there, on the edges of the main stairwell, his hand pressed to his mouth, his eyes pressed to the tiles. "Are you alright?"

He shook his head slightly.

"Oh, darling." She crouched until she came into his view. "Are you lost?"

He shook his head again.

"Ah." She looked around at where they were. "First time in a living city?"

The boy nodded.

"Poor thing. I was a migrant, too. I remember how overwhelming it can be." She rubbed his back soothingly. For a moment, she reminded him of his mother. "It helps if you stop thinking of it as a person."

The boy thanked her and kept climbing.

It was night by the time he found the door leading outside.

It was only work crews up this far. He climbed into a service elevator with some men wearing harnesses and there it was—the pathway to the sky.

He stood and watched the birds drifting over the never-ending desert for a long time. It was never truly dark in the desert, the sand catching onto the light and sending it back into the air like a mist. Far, far away, he could see what looked like a human kneeling on the sand. There would be another if he turned to his right, and another to his left. And if he turned around, he would see the face of this city.

The harnessed crews were already hard at work on the shoulder in front of him, repairing cloth torn by the harsh winds. The city wore beautiful clothes. They were beautiful because he deserved the best, the ministers had told him. They were thick and repaired nightly to protect him from the next day's sun. The only places that were not covered were his marked hand and his face.

Why would he cover his face? the ministers had told him. He's family to everyone.

The boy turned. Then he sat down on the shoulder, looking up at the bare profile. The city's eyes were shut, making him look as if he were asleep. They boy knew that they were sewn that way because the eyeballs had been liquified, that this was done to prevent them from boiling over in the heat. He knew that the stitches were made large as a part of tradition. The ministers had explained it to him in the months after they had chosen the new city. They had told him that these were painless procedures, because the first thing the engineers did was remove the part of his brain that allowed him to feel.

The bareness of the face revealed a small scar—a scar that had once been small, that was now rendered massive, a scar that had once felt personal but now seemed far too public—on the city's chin. The boy had given him that scar. He had bled. It had hurt him enough to make him cry. It was about the same size as some of the stitches.

Their mother had chided him when she found them, crouched together, blood on their hands as they tried desperately to push back in what had already come out. "You're the older brother," she told him. "You need to protect him."

But his father had only laughed. "Brothers get rough," he said. "It's no good to coddle them. This is how family is."

"Violent?" his mother had snapped.

"Complicated." Then he'd winked at the boy. "But you'd better be careful. He might just be bigger than you one day."

The city before him would outlive the boy. Generations would be born within it. They would die in it. They would fall in love, and get married, and build houses and lives in it. This city would teem with life for hundreds of years. His brother would teem with life.

Looking at that familiar smile, at the stitched together eyes, the boy wondered if it was possible for his brother to be alive at all.

He took off his veil. He ripped the pie bag along the seams and laid it out like a tablecloth. He placed both pies on a pile in front of him.

"Since no one else wants any," he told the city.

And the boy began to cry.

Morris Hinkle is a queer, nonbinary writer currently living in the Midwest.

Losing Ground

Varun U. Shetty

After Hokusai's Breaking Waves (Ink on silk)

The sea and the cliff
embrace like wrestlers,
he is   merciless
gutting him with his waves.
Above, the sky is sparse,
and the trees   are blurring in the wind.

What of the lake
at the foot of this cliff?

An audience of clouds gather
and the water leaves in ripples.

A village watches from a distance.

Varun U. Shetty is a writer and critical care physician. He grew up in Mumbai and lives with his partners in Shaker Heights, Ohio. His work has appeared or forthcoming in *Frontier*, *Five South*, *Cleaver*, *Hobart*, *Healing Muse*, *Complete Sentence*, and others. He won the 2022 F. Sean Hodge Prize for Poetry in Medicine. You can read more about him at www.varunushetty.com.

The Sand Knows Its Way Home

L. Chan

The fish eagle catches an updraft on its outstretched wings, momentarily becoming invisible in the glare of the sun, before diving to emerge from the glittering sea with a wriggling fish in its talons. The group of tourists collectively gasps at the display, raising phones and squinting at the cloudless sky. Their photos will be overexposed, the majestic alabaster sweep of the raptor's wing indistinguishable from baby blue sky; the act of preservation distracting them from the bird itself.

Cheng Boon counts the tourists; there are fourteen of them. Fourteen is not a good number; nothing with four is, it sounds like death. Thirteen of them are making noises of appreciation at the wildlife, sweltering under the punishing afternoon glare; one even looks to be unpacking a drone. He sighs and hurries over, the buzz of the drone will frighten the birds. This far from mainland Singapore, with its skyscrapers jousting with the sky, the sounds of humanity are a distant inconvenience for the birds and the crabs of Pulau Semakau. The fourteenth guest catches his eye; the man is about forty, hair prematurely thinning, with the same sun-blasted, salt-scoured complexion that Cheng Boon wears—brown, vellum-like skin that transcended race, all being equal on the sea. The man, like Cheng Boon, is of the tides, even if his faded Metallica t-shirt (a knock-off, the band's name misspelt) and shorts do not distinguish him from the crowd.

The tourists are corralled to the displays showing the sanitised history of the island, and its glorious role in the city it orbits. Semakau is a landfill, stitched together from two islands, cradled by a diaphanous underwater membrane so that the ash of Singapore's effluvia doesn't leach into the sea; against all odds, the birds and the reef creatures have returned. All it cost the country was two villages. Yes, all the villagers moved out and were resettled into government housing, he told an inquisitive teenager. There were a few on this trip, probably doing research for a school project. They nodded at the generosity of the government, the provision of flats with running water and electricity in exchange for the stilted kampung homes in the village of Pulau Semakau. Those new flats were cages of glass, and concrete, and steel. They gently suffocated the spirits of Cheng Boon's father and grandfather; men of the sea who coaxed a living out of the reefs in the shallow waters about Semakau, and who didn't care for the open sky replaced by smooth ceilings, or the breath of the South China Sea replaced by the dull whir of a ceiling fan.

He would have told them that the village of his youth was a small and perfect thing, but what is a small and perfect thing compared to the growing appetite of a nascent mega-city? That appetite was all it took for them to murder a village. This is not the story that the groups come here to listen to, not when they have the sparkling sea before them and the shining city behind. No, they want this thread of the story to be pure and clean, to leave with pictures for Facebook and Instagram, and peeling sunburn to show off in their air-conditioned offices and classrooms. Cheng Boon ushers the group back to the waiting boat as a barge comes by with the day's complement of ash from the incinerators on the mainland. Semakau is an open grave for his boyhood village, and it is still being buried, handful by handful, barge by barge, with funereal ash. He counts the group one last time before he starts the boat. Thirteen. He smiles and leaves a trail of diesel tinted smoke on the water as he returns the group to civilization.

It is forbidden to navigate his small boat between the container ships and tankers plying the southern ports on the southern coast of Singapore. His boat could vanish under the bow of one of those behemoths, be split in two without their crew noticing, be drawn in by the gravity of their mighty propellers and sliced to ribbons. Yet he does it anyway, a minnow amidst whales. In truth, Cheng Boon could have read the waves on a moonless night, feeling the currents merely by the tug on the bow of his tiny boat. Unlike the modern craft he piloted earlier, with its air-conditioned cabin and plush seats, his own boat is a rickety thing of wood, with brittle tires hung around the gunwales to cushion against jetties or other craft. From the jetty, he can see guttering candle flames on the island. Government officials would have tutted, said something about grass fires and handed out a fine from a booklet in triplicate, but Cheng Boon is on no such mission.

Away from the mainland, with the dark of the sea on all sides of the beach, without the glare of electric lights, the sky, with its dusting of stars, felt so close that Cheng Boon could have reached out and touched it. Leaving the mainland for the islands never got old, not for a child of Semakau. He hoists a bag over his shoulder, bottles sweating through the thin canvas, and starts the short hike to the lights on the island.

The man from before has laid out a selection of offerings on sandy ground, illuminated by a semi-circle of candles. Betel nuts, mangoes so sweet and full of juice that there are streaks of sticky fluid dripping from their bases, fragrant flowers and wooden bowls of yellow rice. In the centre, a larger flame on a small metal platter burns, aromatic gum reducing to dark ash.

"I thought I left someone behind," says Cheng Boon.

"I think you knew you did," responds the man, bare to the waist now, sweat running down his back.

"I am Cheng Boon," says Cheng Boon, extending a hand. The stranger takes it. "Affendi," he says.

Cheng Boon offers Affendi a bottle of water and sits on the ground. The other man takes it gratefully; it has been a long day under the sun.

"Terima Kasih, abang," says Affendi. Thank you, brother.

"There has been no keramat ceremony here in many years. Were you from this island?" asks Cheng Boon.

"No, I am from Johor."

"Far from home then. Why would you come to respect my village?"

The other man was silent, the light from the candles casting upwards shadows on his face, the heady smoke from the burning gum resin teasing both their noses. He takes a handful of the sandy ground and lets it trickle out of a closed fist and the wind kisses it on its way to the ground, scattering the sand all the way up the beach. "To make the island, your country bought parts of mine, the flat bottomed boards scraped it from the rivers and the beaches next to the sea. Men came to chase us from our kampung, and they took the ground from beneath our houses."

Cheng Boon nods. The growing city had to be fed, and it ingested man and earth alike. "You are orang laut, then." Sea people.

"Yes, but after the boats scraped sand from around us, the rivers washed away the mangroves. The whole area habis already."

"I am sorry for your loss. When I was a child here, we traded with the orang laut from the straits up north. Mud crabs and catfish from the rivers for squid and snapper from the sea. Haiyah, now everything also need passport."

"Only men need passport," says Affendi. "Wind and wave no need passport. When men gone already, wind and wave will still be here."

"Then why you still here?"

Affendi turns to look at the space beyond his small offering ceremony. "Last time when I go back to the old swamps and rivers, our ancestors gone already. Mangrove gone, ancestor gone. My father was the bomoh for our people; no ancestor, no business. At least I go to school, got Form 6. After school, I found the company that owned the boats, company man said the sand was sold to Singapore. I tried the easier places first. Marina. Changi Airport. Now, I'm here."

Cheng Boon feels an affinity with the spiritualist from Malaysia. They were both people left behind, those who could not get onto the giant unstoppable vehicle of progress, who instead got mangled under its wheels, and in their middle age, could only see it pulling away in the distance, with the rest of the country on its back. "Then our villages died the same way. They moved us from here to flats on the mainland when they needed this island. Our ancestors are here too."

"Do you want to see?" asks Affendi.

Cheng Boon is confused; there was one child in the village who had the sight, but seeing ghosts had its own costs, and the child was always hollow-eyed and sickly. "I don't have that skill."

"I can help, but only for a short while." Affendi leans towards the candles and burning resin, blowing out the fire on the gum gently and raising a smattering of ash and embers. He presses his thumb into the ash and walks over to where Cheng Boon is seated. There are no night birds or crickets on the island, no sound but the rhythmic lap of waves on sand. Cheng Boon closes his eyes as Affendi smears warm ash over his eyelids, and then another smear on his forehead. When he opens his eyes again, he sees them all.

They glow gently in the dark, the remnants of the village of Pulau Semakau. Cheng Boon can recognize some of them, older aunties and uncles, but echoes of their former lives. He could almost see the village of his youth, houses of wood perched on stilts, with sloped roofs of zinc. The houses were all around the tide line, at times the sea would even lap at the front doors. But the structures were long gone, only the people remained, some aged, some young, neither fully of this world or the next. Here too were strangers from across the sea, dressed in simple sarongs, carrying the tools of fishermen: nets, hooks for boats, traps for crabs. Affendi's people. His people. Both here on the island, lost spirits. The ghosts are gathered around Affendi's ceremony, drawn by the sweet smoke and offerings. It is clear to Cheng Boon that despite the circumstances of their lives and deaths, the two groups know each other in the hereafter. They exchange cordial smiles and greetings as they assemble around the only two living people on the island.

"Thank you. For showing me," says Cheng Boon, and the wind is cooler on his cheeks for the tears that it dries. "It's been a long time since anybody has offered anything to the spirits here."

Affendi makes as though to clear off the ceremony, but Cheng Boon stops him. "Let them stay a little longer," he says. And they sit for a while longer, in the company of spirits.

"You know, Chinese believe that we can burn offerings for the dead, and the riches will be transferred to the afterlife," says Cheng Boon.

"Some of my people believe that things that are respected and loved have spirits."

The two of them look to the jetty.

The boat has been in Cheng Boon's family since before he was born, though little enough remains of the original. Panels have been ripped out and replaced, the engine has been overhauled. But it was his father's boat, and now it is his. Both men worked to empty a large plastic can of fuel about the deck. The two men stand knee-deep in the calm sea, watching. Cheng Boon should have felt something when he sees the flames licking the deck, spreading along the salt-infused wood and burning blue and green with the flaking paint. The boat is the last thing of his village that he owns. The sole physical link to his youth and roots. But he will continue bringing tourists here, continue telling them the sanctioned history of the island. He glances away from the fire, and looks at the other man, a stranger to him until hours ago, but now siblings in an old, nameless grief. What common name can there be for the depredations of the many on the few?

"Look," says Affendi. The fire has bitten deep into the boat, the frame is crumbling into itself, and soon it will start taking on water. But there is still a little of the magic of the ash in his eyes, and Cheng Boon can still see the ghosts, both of his villagers and Affendi's, all the peoples of the sea. Like the two men, the ghosts are knee-deep in the water. There is something happening to the boat, even as it burns and fractures into the water—there is a shadow of it left, a ghost of a boat, and the old spirits are already beginning to clamber aboard.

"We will get into trouble for this tomorrow, you know," says Cheng Boon.

"So kesian that your old boat caught fire when you came back to check on the island to find a lost tourist, very hardworking," says Affendi.

"Thank you for letting me see them again."

"Thank you for the boat. I wonder where the ghosts will go?"

There was no changing the past, not for either village. The present serves too many the way it is. There is no atoning for a past denied. The future, now the future is malleable. There can be peace for the dead, a way for the ghosts to take to the waves again. No restitution without sacrifice; a debt had to be paid. Cheng Boon had never been far from Semakau, neither in his youth nor when he found his job. But he has something new now. A new story, for tomorrow's tourists, maybe. About a ghost ship, crewed by spirits from Singapore and Malaysia alike, plying the waters. Cheng Boon smiles and waits for the sun to rise on a new day.

L CHAN hails from Singapore. He spends most of his time wrangling a team of two dogs, Mr Luka and Mr Telly. His work has appeared in places like *Clarkesworld*, *Translunar Travellers Lounge*, *Podcastle*, *The Dark,* and he was a finalist for the 2020 Eugie Foster Memorial Award. He tweets inordinately @lchanwrites.

Great Barrier Reef

Justine Norton-Kertson

Turns out poetic justice
—for me anyway—
might mean
dying in a flood.

At age twelve
I had the privilege
of swimming in The Great Barrier Reef.
Floating among dayglow coral,
a psychedelic spacewalk
through old growth aquatic forest.

At age forty
I met myself there
and asked him if
two thousand, seven hundred pounds of CO2
was worth it.

I screamed until
my face caught fire;
we only heard
the sound of bubbles
drifting to the surface
as if time
didn't have a care in the world.

The ocean suffers.
Schools of rainbow fish
swirl in sync toward extinction.
Coral withers wishing
it could evolve fins.

Justine Norton-Kertson (they/she/he) is an author, gamemaker, musician, and community organizer. Their work has been featured in magazines including Utopian Science Fiction Magazine and Jupiter Review. She is editing a solarpunk anthology for AK Press and his lunarpunk anthology, *Bioluminescent*, is forthcoming in January 2023 from Android Press. Their nonfiction book, *Solarpunk Witchcraft*, is forthcoming from Microcosm Publishing in 2024. She can be found on Twitter @jankwrites.

Reconciliation

Sara E. Palmer

When you really want to break someone,
you take their kids.

We're a simple animal, and bearing costs.

After the storm I go down the beach,
visit time, lenses of shell on shell,
thousands of practical years of
canoes and oysters, fires on the sand,
veils of cedar and the red bark of madrones
bright against the bluffs.
I call a guy I know from the tribe and we walk it, together,
eroding our way down the tideline,
sand in our socks.
It's as big as we always thought it had to be,
if we ever saw it, which of course now we are.
The water's rising, unstoppably.
Waves are breaking around our ankles.

We don't have a design plan
for cheerful interpretive signage
about community heritage
when the end of history
is, here's where your priests
took our kids and held them captive
and wouldn't let us see our own children.
And, here's where our priests
took your children, so they could *get an education.*
Now it's a park!
We have all learned a lot, since then;
we have not learned enough to teach this.

Even if we could come up with a way
to word it, someone's going to come along

some Sunday afternoon, with a paint marker,
and draw a mustache or maybe a dick
over the plastic-covered portrait
of someone else's grandfather.

We're standing on this beach in the rain,
watching history slosh out into the bay
to mix with dredge spoils
and abandoned vessels
and everything else the city would like to sink.

We climb back up to the parking lot
where we turn our keys and burn some hydrocarbons,
making everything just a tiny bit worse.
Two old ravens, tempest-tossed, half-seen, creaking,
land on the strand behind us,
scaly feet gritty with forgotten truths,
comfortable lies,
and the bones that wash out of creek banks
when nobody is watching.

Sara E. Palmer is an archaeologist with the State of Washington. Her poetry was recently called "conversational and aloof, sharp and personal", which is about what she's like, too. She lives in the woods and keeps children, animals, and an unreasonable number of books in a house in Olympia.

A Glass of You

Filomena Acosta

"This is my home," my mother says to me one overcast day.

Picture this: mother and daughter are sitting on the couch together, our ponchos pooling and swallowing us whole. We are looking at a picture on the internet, a snapshot of the valley in Petorca. My mother was born in that Chilean city, a tiny bird nestled in the bosom of the Andes, gasping through thin air and an ever-evolving awe of the world. I expect, watching her then, a cloud of nostalgia to fog her eyes, for her to fly away from me and the couch here in Canada.

She does not fly away. I notice her speech warbles with hesitation, her throat holding that last word down, home, dragging it out long and narrow like the country. How I remember her staring, the rubbing of her eyes, the drugstore eyedrops, and the small circle of her mouth.

When she finally says it again—"This is my home"—no longer is it a statement, rather a climb, peaking in a question. She leaves me behind then to dash to the safe upstairs, rummaging through our family's birth certificates and citizen papers and passports and who knows what, until she brings back to me an old picture.

My fingers retain still the feeling of that smooth, glossy paper; of how I turn it, checking the back to see ink splotches faded with time:

Lxxx, Petorca, 1975.

Wistfulness, I understand then, means there is some semblance of a home to yearn for. There is still something there to return to—yes, there could be little differences here and there—but you can walk the land and observe, with tinted sunglasses, a kaleidoscope of memories and endless futures gleaming in the sunset.

Nothing of that nature is found in the photograph in her hands—it is a reality which does not exist anymore. It was, as I consider the image, something beautiful, with swathes of green and yellow and blue. It was, she tells me, the place she was happiest in, even if she did not have hot water or had to use an outhouse or went hungry. It is, as I discover, somehow, the same place as the cracked, parched desert on the internet labelled *Petorca*. The jarring combination of speaking, of thinking, all at once present, past, and unknown, makes for an ominous blanket heavier than the warmest poncho.

This is my home? This cannot be my home. Did I ever have one? I had one, I know I did, once, but it is not this. How long can the world go on for? How long can I?

"What happened to the river?" I say, taking the role of the fool who asks obvious questions before a disaster foretold.

I remember the soft curve of her jaw as she cranes her head to our popcorn ceiling, going past it to enter something holy and safe.

"God help us all," she responds.

What can one say about the environment that has not already been said? How could we reconcile with the fact that the place we were born will not be the same place we will die, even if the maps, even if our hearts, say otherwise?

My old university here in Canada floats on top of a marsh. I can feel the chill of the mornings I've spent walking along watery pathways, frogs croaking and salamanders whirling near my feet; occasionally, on these walks, my eyes wandered to the trail of smoke that wafts up from the clanging industrial parts of the city. Group projects in my academic career consisted of developing apps that would help the user report turtles crushed and splattered by cars, to hopefully have someone help take them to wildlife rescues. My lectures had many students yawning through the degradation of our Great Lakes, a source of life, with algae blooms and gifts of spewing sewage and oil spills.

At these institutions, one looks at the *data*; one maps and calculates and writes obligatory reflections that are more opinion pieces on the reality of things, and then one moves on. Moving on commonly means a hiring event where major oil and mining companies, among others in little cliques of giggling imperialistic friends, gather us ready and bright-eyed, one by one.

A funny thing: my tía abuela, Juana, a stout woman in her

nineties, still works to run a family goat farm in Chile. My tía sends my mother a video of the old woman on the news, appearing on the screen with hands curling like tendrils in a garden.

"No way," I say, looking at the old woman in amazement, seeing a continent of toughness etched on her pixelated face. "She's still alive?"

My mother slaps me before she starts the clip again, leaning in, trying to listen to her tía's words carefully.

Petorca province is a major provider of that emerald jewel of a fruit, the avocado—la palta—which can only grow in certain regions. A *just right* environment is mandatory for the fussy fruit. Raising them requires 320 litres of water per avocado. Agricultural companies and politicians and the like illegally divert the coursing river to these fields. Once grown, they are exported to a European or North American country, a destiny coded on stickers and red-flag sale signs, all to end up part of people's self care smoothie or a sandwich in a bougie restaurant.

There, on television, my tía abuela Juana speaks of the town's water crisis: people cannot wash their clothes, they cannot take showers, crops are wilting, livestock dying from dehydration. She could not afford to buy the avocados that her neighbours grow. She is still alive, yes, todo bien gracias a Dios, but who knows about the well-being of her children, many who work at the farm, if all her goats die from no water? What about her grandchildren; her great great-great-grandchildren; her great-great-great-great-great-great-great grandchildren?

In the climate crisis, it is those *at risk*—ones statistically contributing the least to global pollution and energy consumption—who will encounter the worst effects of it. Though I believe that designating those *at risk* is to make the sacrificial lamb a matter of inheritance, instead of the truth of chronic disenfranchisement, of intentional displacement. Everything has a price to it, and some people are willing to be paid. Even the world burning has a price.

In Chile, Patagonian fluvial systems, running like veins to the end of the world, suffer as their ecosystems are upset by deforestation and pollution. Lithium exploitation in the name of green electromobility in turn consumes water in the north, with mining sites near primarily Indigenous communities. In my home here in Canada, water still has material needs we must provide, a necessary relationship that the media calls *disruptive* and *violent* and *holding this country back*. The water does not need oil spills and fertilizer pollution and waste; it does not need to water golf courses or suburban lawns or mall fountains; it does not need people to face police brutality for protesting these violations.

There are things to say about Indigenous sovereignty. There are things to say on how the fight against colonisation is the fight for water justice. There are things to say about our power as a group of people, that through each home we love, those which are fracturing like cracks in clay, we make our attempts at resilience. We survive. Fight.

I do not write about this for the love of writing about this. I do not write believing I have a voice that is good or matters above the rest. Those things to say on environmental justice perhaps are said better by others instead of me: an overwrought, disabled, neurotic Latina, with a persistent fear of misstepping hovering over me like a fly. However, now is the time where we must drive our purpose towards the collective needs of our people, and to the land.

I laugh when someone asks me if I consider myself an academic or a writer. It is unnatural for me in those ecosystems. What is there for people in that hierarchy of beings, with those intellectuals that love to create and fondle and debate among each other? However, I do consider myself an eternal student, and read anything that could explain the seedlings of questions that sprout from my chest: what is justice, what is the environment, who are we all in between?

Taking an Indigenous Knowledge class, I loved my time there, my professor almost lulling me with stories and exciting me in challenging the normative way of thinking, even when it was difficult at times. There I read and analysed, as part of our curriculum, Robin Wall Kimmerer's book *Braiding Sweetgrass*.

"Wow," I wrote to my professor late in the evening, happy to see the poetry in the world around us translated to words I could finally comprehend. "She's just like me. For real!"

I believe the part of the book I just must write about goes like this, after introducing the reader to the Onondaga Thanksgiving Address: "Each person, human or no, is bound to every other in a reciprocal relationship. Just as all beings have a duty to me, I have a duty to them. If an animal gives its life to feed me, I am in turn bound to support its life. If I receive a stream's gift of pure water, then I am responsible for returning a gift in kind. An integral part of a human's education is to know those duties and how to perform them."

A great achievement of colonialism is that it convinces people that hyper-individualism is good. That there is not a right to anything unless you buy it. This is seen in Chile, with waters regulated by private property laws, which are a symptom of the infection of neoliberalism, implemented after the coup of 1973. For how could one *own* water? Why do government officials hand water out on a first-come first-served basis? The delusion of hyper-individualism creates the mantra *this is just the way things are*, that it is natural for an old woman to go on television and plead for water in the community and to stop desecrating the land she was born on.

It cannot be an individual's responsibility to save watery ecosystems and the turtles by banning straws; we cannot turn up our nose at disabled people's need for plastic straws and not do a thing to, say, fast fashion companies overflowing landfills and causing water pollution with last micro-season's trends. It is abhorrent that the average person's carbon footprint is always scrutinized, yet a celebrity can use private jets to fly mere minutes on a whim. There is a need for community. There is a duty we must fulfill to each other and the land.

Because for what, for whom, do we declare environmental justice?

There may not be a complete reversal of the climate crisis. That opportunity may very likely wave us by. Unprecedented times are precedent-setting times. Yet it is still within our power to continue forward. I do not mean that we all hold hands together and sing *la-la-de-da*, because there are those that oppose what needs to be done. There are those who will say that this injustice, these crises, are not real, even when we look at them in our own backyards. I also do not mean that progress, even technological progress, is bad, for there are things like ecological socialism to take into consideration as we move forward, ever forward. There is no one solution that may tie up neatly in a bow; we must think of the tangible, we must think of each other, and not fall into traps of ecofascism or relentless nihilism.

We live in a perfect green and blue spaceship. This is our

home. We are born here, of course we will take care of it, one way or another.

After we watch the news and say our goodbyes to my tía, my mother and I prepare food together. She speaks of childhood memories while baking fresh bread; I simmer with the squash soup in all the ways I feel helpless—and all the ways I feel hopeful—about my power in this world.

When I sit with my family at the dinner table, that precious glass of water stays by my hand, waiting to give me a gift, and I accept it in each swallow. *Tomorrow*, I think to myself, *tomorrow I'll return the gift, in full.*

While forks scrape plates and conversations lull, my mind drifts away: to snowy peaks and pine trees and endless sky. I remember the smell of the sea, the sun on my back, the green of the valley. I dream of mountain goats following at the heels of an old woman. I see the happiness that land gave my mother in her smile.

But what about the river? Its silence now is louder than the rush of water ever was. I hope our children hear its song again, one day. I hope our children have a glass of you, dear river.

Pero todos bien gracias a Dios, y mi gente.

References

Wall Kimmerer, R. (2013). *Braiding Sweetgrass: Indigenous Wisdom, Scientific Knowledge, and the Teaching of Plants*. Milkweed Editions.

Filomena Acosta is a Chilean (Andean and Mapuche descent) 2nd generation Canadian living in the Halton Region. She was on the longlist for the CBC Nonfiction Short Story Prize for 2022, and her speculative work could be seen in *Augur Magazine*. When not writing, she bides her time being a researcher at her local library and wondering what she will eat for dinner. You can find her at @emicawrites8 on Twitter.

Sublease of Land

J. H. Lee

I come from another ocean
just as deep, just as mazarine

with tides that swell and churn
of cloves, anise, cardamom,

a constellation. Where north?
Where east? A foreboding task

for someone so close
to the equator.

Do not drown. Do not drown.
A leatherback turtle

clutches together
an archipelago just for you.

In a hushed patois,
you gill fish and hem

layers upon layers upon layers
of waxed orchids and peacocks

whose three thousand and one blue
eyes quake, crest, verge in a wave.

I am wrecked, wreckage,
my feet knead water, my feet,

alien fin, sublease of land.

J. H. Lee hails from the Malay Archipelago and has lived in North America and East Africa. He thinks, writes, and imagines in several languages but only dreams in three. He is currently writing a book about humans and rodents in Tanzania.

Yellow River Burial

Floris M. Kleijne

It was Bobby's last wish to be composted and spread over their vegetable patch above the Yellow River, just a couple of miles upstream of its confluence with the Mississippi. They grew peas, eggplant, tomatoes there; firm, tasty lettuce, cauliflower, and kale; even a patch of wheat that yielded symbolic amounts of flour, but that Bobby had been passionate about. The rich alluvial soil of the riparian required no fertilization to speak of, and hardly any irrigation, but Bobby had dreamt of resting among his crops, of living on in next year's harvest.

The vegetable garden sat where the sloping grass leveled out before plunging down into the fecund abundance of the riparian proper. The garden bathed in sunlight throughout the day in most seasons, and Bobby and Alfonso had spent many an afternoon lying in the grass overlooking the rows of pea stalks and the low, cobbled width of the kale crops, drying and basking in the hot summer rays after swimming the calm flow of the river.

Al stares out of the study window at the garden across the river, a medical bill with hiragana and English printing clutched in his arthritic hand.

He had never expected Bobby to be the first to go.

His husband had always been stubborn about his health, both when all doctors had still been human and now that RD-TDs, Robotic Diagnostics and Treatment Devices, had mostly displaced the traditional white coats and stethoscopes. He rarely fell ill, and even when he did, he'd sooner cross the river for fresh vegetables than go to their GP for a pharmaceutical solution.

So when his eyes developed a yellow cast, and later, when sharp, stabbing pains in his stomach made him double over, he'd shrugged and cooked some kale.

"I'll be fine," he said, holding Alfonso's gaze with yellowed eyes as Al argued through his tears.

"You can't know that. You keep saying that our house isn't medical, that it could be wrong. But it could be right, Bobby. Not just about the hep, but about the cirrhosis, about the liver cancer even. What if our house is right?"

Bobby squeezed Al's hand and shrugged.

"Then we've had a good run, sweetheart. Who would have thought we'd get to our golden wedding? Not your parents, that's for sure. Or mine, for that matter."

They had chuckled in unison, until Bobby's laughter turned into a coughing fit. Al had helped him sit up straight and adjusted his pillow. Together, they had watched through the panoramic bedroom window as the sun set over the Yellow River.

Bobby had been right. They'd had a good run. But even after fifty years, he was gone too soon.

And now Alfonso can't even fulfill his last wish.

REMAINS DISPOSAL QUESTIONNAIRE - ROBERT "BOBBY" REOLIN

Please answer the below questions completely and truthfully and correct any information already provided. Withholding or misrepresenting information that may affect the disposal of your loved one's remains is a class-3 misdemeanor under the Funerary Environmental Impact Act (FEIA) and will result in an automatic determination of Reuse.

1. The cause of death for your loved one is registered as:

COMPLICATIONS FROM AN UNTREATED HEPATITIS C INFECTION

The medication your loved one was taking at the time of their demise is listed as:

NONE

Please enter any information concerning the cause of death not included in this description, and/or list any medication they were using that might affect the disposal of their remains.

Al smooths the Japanese medical bill on the desk surface. Such a little thing, really. Bobby's dental had covered all of it. Such a little thing, with such major consequences.

He sighs and gets up from the form-fitting desk chair with a grunt. Grabbing his coat from the rack by the front door, he makes a stop in the garage to rummage through their toolbox. He unplugs the Mazda from the charging socket and buzzes down their wooded driveway, taking Route 401 into town. He may be too late. The disposal director may already have processed Bobby. He may be too late, but he may just be on time.

All he needs is five minutes alone with Bobby.

It's very rare these days to get a composting permit. It has grown as uncommon as burial and even cremation, what with all the prosthetics and chemo. For the thousandth time, Al wonders: how much of Bobby's refusal of treatment was prompted by his desire to be spread over their vegetable patch?

2. Please select your preferred method of disposal of your loved one's remains.

X Composting - By selecting this option, you apply for a composting and fertilization permit under FEIA.

0 Burial - By selecting this option, you apply for a burial permit under FEIA.

0 Cremation - The per-Lb fee for fuel and for carbon dioxide compensation will be calculated from the weight of the remains at the time of cremation. By selecting this option, you commit to paying this fee in full.

If the above options are greyed out, it means that medication, artificial bodily enhancements, and/or prosthetics present in the deceased's body at the time of their demise as registered in the Central Administration of Medical Procedures (CAMP), preclude composting, burial and cremation. In that case, please select Reuse below.

0 Reuse - This may include, but is not limited to: organ transplant, scientific research, trace element reclamation, food production, and construction (primarily bones). If you select this option, please also select one of the previous ones for those body parts that turn out to be unsuitable for reuse.

The parking lot at the Disposal Home is almost full. There must be a ceremony in progress. Al hopes it will make his job easier. In a practical sense, that is; emotionally, he's afraid this will be one of the hardest things he's ever done.

When he enters the lobby, the receptionist recognizes him and gets up with a flustered look uncharacteristic of the disposal profession.

"Mr. Reolin, one moment." She disappears into the back and returns with the familiar, kind figure of Mrs. Ahenny. Mrs. Ahenny rounds the reception desk and takes Al's hand in both her own.

"Alfonso, it's good to see you. I was just processing your beloved Robert's composting application...." A look of concern draws across her face, and Al's heart sinks. Is he too late? She guides him to a conference room, all subdued colors and monochrome flowers. They sit at a low table.

"Is everything in order?" Al asks, but he already knows the answer.

"Well...." Mrs. Ahenny places her fingertips together and gazes earnestly into his eyes. "Of course, we've discussed dear Robert's deeply felt wish to be spread over your lovely vegetable garden. As you know, the FEIA is very clear on the rules and regulations surrounding composting. And I was processing your response to question 3 in the disposal questionnaire and assessing dear Robert's earthly remains...."

That's it. They have found it. They have found it, which

means that as far as Mrs. Ahenny knows, he has lied in the questionnaire. The automatic misdemeanor conviction isn't the worst of it, not by a long shot. Al feels his tears starting to run as he realizes that any chance of a composting permit is now lost. Mrs. Ahenny has no choice but to report him, and Bobby will not rest in his beloved garden above the river. His remains will be processed for reuse.

The pliers in Al's jacket pocket are useless now.

`3. Please list any prosthetics, bodily enhancements, and/or other artificial items and materials that would prohibit composting. To obtain a composting permit, all of these items need to be removed prior to disposal director assessment. According to the CAMP, the following items are known to be in the deceased's body:`

`NONE`

Al remembers their trip to Japan, the remarkable range of delicious foods, the terraces overlooking Kamo River, the cherry blossoms, the overwhelming beauty of the temples... and the acute pain that had all but incapacitated Bobby. It had been one of the few times Bobby had ever submitted to visiting a medical professional. The Japanese dentist had performed an efficient root canal, and Bobby had felt no pain for the remainder of their vacation.

Back Stateside, Bobby had had every intention of reporting the procedure to the CAMP. But administration had always been Al's responsibility in their marriage. So of course, it got forgotten.

Until Al found the bill in Bobby's desk yesterday.

If he had remembered, or if he had gone through Bobby's papers before filling out the questionnaire, he could have mentioned the composite filling under question 3. He would gladly have paid the fee to have it removed.

Too late now.

"Mr. Reolin?"

Al sits up with a start, realizing Mrs. Ahenny has been speaking to him for some time.

"Sorry, what was that?"

She smiles.

"As I was saying, when we assess a loved one's remains, we sometimes discover foreign items that were overlooked or forgotten, and thus accidentally left out of the questionnaire. Quite often, it's nothing more serious than a molar with composite filling." She pauses and looks him in the eyes. "If they were disclosed in the questionnaire, we would of course remove them; we have the tools right there, in an unlocked cabinet in the mourning room. But if the questionnaire doesn't mention those items, FEIA requires us to report the omission, and to deny composting."

She gets up and folds her hands in front of her. Al looks up at her with grief and dread. He is so certain what she'll say that when she does speak he has to play her words back in his mind twice before he understands. And when he does understand, relief floods his eyes as he hugs her in gratitude.

"Would you like to spend some more time with your beloved Robert in the mourning room, while I prepare the composting permit?"

The glass facade of their home reflects the splendid, riotous sunset. Darkness will soon descend over the valley. The smell of grass and soil is loud and strong in the air, a scent Bobby used to love. The birds have already grown silent, and Al hears only the quiet murmur of the river and the wind whispering in the spruces above the house.

He kneels in the soil beside Bobby's memorial and rubs some of the rich, fertile clay between his fingers. His gaze drifts over the garden. He sees Bobby's ruddy cheeks in the curve of the tomatoes; the blond locks of his youth in the waving of golden stalks. Al knows he is being fanciful, but he deserves some fancy.

He turns to the marble monument and brushes off the splashes of mud from last night's rainstorm. The words 'In loving memory' at the top of the stone are untouched by the mud, but Al takes special care to clean the carved letters of Bobby's name. He straightens up with popping knees and surveys the result.

Something still mars the surface of the headstone. A drop of mud is covering the dot in their last name, the 'i' in 'Reolin' an irregular brown splash. Al bends over and gently brushes the last mud away.

The white, knobby ivory in the half-inch dot sparkles in the reflected sunset.

"There," Al says. "There you are."

Floris M. Kleijne writes stories, some of them award-winning, in the interstices between his family, his day job, and his insatiable craving for Netflix binges. His stories have appeared in the *Writers of the Future* anthologies, *Daily Science Fiction*, *Galaxy's Edge*, and numerous other publications. As Floris Kleijne, without the middle initial—yes, he's an Iain (M.) Banks fan—he is also an award-winning Dutch thriller writer. He lives in a centuries old farm house in the Dutch river district, with a wonderful wife, two cheerful sons, a nosy tabby, twelve crates of Legos, and thousands of books. This is his third appearance in *Reckoning*. Find more of his writing on https://www.floriskleijne.com.

How to Place an Intravenous Line

Cristina Legarda

The Atlantic horseshoe crab, *Limulus polyphemus,*
is not a crab at all—
more an ancient, armored spider,
here 500 million years.

> *Choose the right vessel: long and straight.*
> *Choose a good insertion point: key to success.*
> *Tourniquet, swab, stab, advance,*
> *occlude, connect, untie, secure:*
> *the sequence for an intravenous line.*

Horseshoe crab blood is blue
from copper in hemocyanin.
Amoebocytes in the blood
detect bacteria in drugs, implants,
electrolyte solutions—anything destined
to enter our bloodstream.

> *Needle tip in—*
> *backflow of blood*
> *into the cannula barrel—*
> *drop your angle, advance a bit more,*
> *then slide the catheter*
> *smoothly into the vein.*

After blood harvest
Horseshoe crabs move less, mate less.

A third will perish.

With fewer horseshoe crab eggs to eat, grackles
and loggerhead turtles waste away; red knots

flying from Tierra del Fuego to the Arctic Circle
drop in numbers by the thousands.

There should be a word for the triumph we feel
when we see the flash of red blood
in the barrel. Invasion. Proof.
In hoc signo vinces.

The name Polyphemus—Poseidon's giant, one-eyed son—
means "abounding in songs and legends",
but all we've done to *Limulus polyphemus* is use it
for fertilizer, whelk bait, and blood.

60,000 dollars a gallon
for limulus amoebocyte lysate
to test I.V. fluids. We almost never think
of the cost in lives and ecosystems, the martyrs
destroyed to get us here, how entitled we feel
to bleed the world.

In Japan, horseshoe crabs, *Tachypleus tridentatus*,
are Taira samurai reborn. Male crabs attach themselves
to female mates, and they move around together,
an asymmetric pair encoded into local parlance
as a love ideal, *kabutogani-no-chigiri*,
horseshoe crab commitment.

We need a word
for the debt we owe
the creatures we exploit,
an unholy grail
stained blue
with our saviors' blood.

At the far end of the wrack line:
an overturned horseshoe crab,
book gills open to the sky,
chelicerae motionless,
vulnerable as Prometheus

but lifeless and dry
on the sand, worthless
even to ravenous gulls.

Cristina Legarda was born in the Philippines and spent her early childhood there before moving to Bethesda, Maryland. She is now a practicing physician in Boston. Her work has appeared in *America* magazine, *The Dewdrop*, *Plainsongs*, *FOLIO*, *Ruminate*, *The Good Life Review*, and others.

History of Orconectes

Dyani Sabin

I
In ethanol, the chitin of a crayfish fades,
a carapace of rubber and silk.
Its joints articulate, tail spreads under pressure, uropods from telson
under a microscope, the jaggedness of its mouthparts, a question.

The lab is silent as I inspect ten-legged aliens, door open for fumes.
Is preservation respect for the dead?

II
November, I am split, cephelothorax cracked and my innards exposed;
the crayfish lab is open, wide enough to scurry in.
My professor wears pearl earrings, *Hyriopsis schlegelii;*
Emma is dead.

Keys pressed in my hand, teeth coarse, uneven, an answer,
Be as busy as you need.
Janitors whistle in the hall at midnight, so I don't startle when the door opens.
    Trash empty, *get some sleep kid.*
The dead aliens do not speak;
pink sunrise lends them the specter of rusty shells and coral swimmerets.

III
Orconectes rusticus, native to Kentucky,
crossed the continental divide to the Ohio River watershed,
borne in a fisherman's bucket.
    What journey would that be?
    Excised from your life by rough hands,
your friends, strung up as bait, vanish.
Dumped into a new stream, alone.

Did they mourn?

IV
Ecosystems collapse, streams stripped clean of algae, fish, insects,
a river-shaped void.
Even as they crossbreed,
Orconectes sanbornii is outcompeted by rusty invaders.
Evolutionary survival, the passage of genes
to future generations;
a poor measure of life.

V
Dust coats azure sky, endless corn to the left, soybeans to the right.
We stop the van at a culvert.
Between rocks, in the riffles, the species roam.
Barehanded, I can catch Orconectids.
Left spooks them backwards into my right.
My grip solid on the carapace, a chela swings to pinch my thumb.
Iron smell in the mud. I bleed, rust red on the river stones.

VI
Captured, I break off a leg segment and release my crustacean.
Each leg deposited in cell lysis solution. Each molt brings new legs.
    It survives. Do crayfish feel pain?

In the tarot, the crayfish represents greatness, our higher calling.
A tray of legs on the passenger seat, I listen to the wind in the corn,
drive until dusk, moon peach-ripe on the horizon.

VII
The limbs—in blue, fingertip-sized test tubes—like a memory
fragmented.

Dyani Sabin is an author of speculative fiction, poetry, and science journalism. Her work has been published in *Strange Horizons*, *Enchanted Conversations*, *Vastarien*, as well as *National Geographic*, and *Popular Science*. You can find her haunting a cornfield, chasing ghosts on the endangered species list, or on Twitter @DyaniSabin.

A Scarcity of Sharks

Kelsea Yu

Bruce is seventeen feet long and would've weighed around two tons when he was murdered by a trophy hunter. Killing rare creatures for sport is supposed to be a relic of the past now that most of the world's wild animals are some level of endangered. But for some, the desire to prove something runs deeper than the fear of punishment. Thanks to a bartender's tip about a local bachelor party bragging about plans to go shark hunting, the Marine Conservation Enforcement Guard made it to the dock in time to confiscate the kill. A year in jail and ten thousand dollars later, Bruce's murderer has apparently paid his debt to society, but it was too late for this white shark.

And, maybe, for all of the white sharks. Only two sightings have been reported in the past three years, neither confirmed by experts. Scientists have been shouting for decades that we're killing an estimated 97–99% of our ocean's apex predators, and now that we might actually have done it, there are suddenly rallying cries. Humans love to begin caring about an animal as soon as it's about to be wiped from the planet. Too bad that by then, there's almost nothing we can do about it.

But with Bruce, whose body was flash preserved and taken to a conservation lab for immediate regrowth, we're trying anyway.

We can't reanimate him, or grow a new Bruce. It's too complicated. We've never had enough specimens to fully understand shark biology, and full-body cloning laws are prohibitive enough that it would take us years just to get the go-ahead to try.

But we can grow new insides for a simulacrum using synth-muscle tech that was developed for prosthetics, faux cartilaginous skeletal elements, and sensory organs grown in Petri dishes. All housed in Bruce's own skin, more permanently preserved than the rest of him.

The result is, well . . . about as much like a shark as the new human-skinned androids (now available in your choice of skin tone!) are to people. One more reminder that we need to save the actual sharks, or this is all we'll have left.

But, hell, we worked hard on Bruce. He can swim like a shark, he can use most of a shark's senses, and best of all? He can interface with a human mind—my mind, once we finish the security procedures.

As usual, I go through the checklist with Callista, one item at a time. *Any gaps or fit issues with the skinsuit? No. Reoxybreather diagnostics? Green light. Interface fluid tank? Full. Core temp control air system? Working properly. Intravenous regulation line? Secure.* And then I'm in the chamber at the heart of Bruce's body, curled up like a fetus. Ready to be reborn a shark.

Callista hands me the breathing tube and face mask, and I expect the cool practicality of her fingers brushing back my hair and placing the wired nodes. But it's Deng's voice, low and solemn, that calls out gently instead. "Let me do it."

She doesn't argue or make a snide remark, and I'm grateful, even as my heart speeds up. If she can see it on her diagnostics screen, she keeps it to herself.

His fingers, rough and callused from the rigors of our daily work, run through my hair as gently as he can manage. He strokes my hair slowly and deliberately, and for a moment, I can't breathe, my mind filling with *what-ifs*. If he hadn't sworn off love after his husband died in a car accident the year before I met him. If we'd both gotten a little drunker that one *almost* night in the lab last autumn. If we hadn't dedicated every moment of our waking lives to Bruce, to finding the last white sharks left in the world. To saving *Carcharodon carcharias*.

He draws in a breath, about to say something, and the world stops for one moment, full of potential.

And then he coughs, a sound that catches in his throat, and I hear him gulp before he whispers, "Come back to me, safe and whole, okay?"

He doesn't add *I couldn't bear it if you didn't* or anything that dramatic. But it's more than he's ever dared say before, and I tuck away the memory of his words.

Come back to me.

"I will," I whisper back.

He places the nodes and helps me adjust the breathing tube and face mask. Then the chamber closes, and I hear Callista's disembodied voice in my head.

Are you ready?

Yes, I reply by thinking the words forcefully.

The chamber fills with interface fluid as Callista double-checks everything before zipping up Bruce's skin.

The water parts for me as I glide through it in Bruce's body, perfectly designed for the element to which humans are so ill-suited. As with all thunniform sharks, I need only bend my tail from side to side to propel myself forward at incredible speeds. It doesn't matter that I've been in the body of this shark more times than my age; I find myself marveling at the raw power in my synthmuscular tail, the flexibility in my skin. Creatures so perfectly built for the ocean that they've survived everything this planet threw at them for millions of years.

Everything except humans.

I try to shove the thought aside, to let myself have a few minutes of wild, unbridled joy. I'm here. I'm really here, in the open ocean, as close to being a shark as anyone has ever become. This is my reward for every afternoon in the simulator, swimming faux seas. This is what I thought about on the long nights spent circling the tank in the aquarium after hours. This is what I dreamed of as we spent the last two weeks at an inlet, Callista and Deng keeping watch while I familiarized myself with a piece of the ocean.

I dash ahead, looking around at the vibrant life around me. Fish that scatter as my bulk approaches, neon specs that blur below me as I blow by them, until Callista's voice tells me to *slow down!* We're giddy at seeing the things we've dreamt of seeing up close. I slow down, swimming toward the ocean floor for a closer look.

Don't descend too fast, Callista reminds me, and I hate that for a moment, in the joy of discovery, I've forgotten. This isn't like diving; not exactly. The preservation fluid, readouts from the nodes, and intravenous lines snaking into my arms cushion much of the risk of internal pressure building to dangerous levels. And it helps that my mind is the only part of me that's awake to connect with Bruce. Technically, my human body is asleep, which means I can't panic and gulp in air or hold my breath, both lead contributors to diver deaths.

Still, despite the advantages we've built into Bruce's body, it doesn't hurt to be cautious when we're paving new ground. I slow my descent, scanning the area both to give myself a clear look at the wonders beneath me and to offer Callista and Deng the footage they're both craving. In a shallower pocket of ocean, psychedelic purple nudibranchs covered in neon orange quills crawl by, their squirmy bodies swaying with the rippling water. Wolf eels dart out of their hideouts in a rocky reef. A lobster sporting honey-colored spots snaps long pincers as it scurries away from me.

Got your fill? I ask Callista. Her *yes* response is followed by a contented sigh. *Carry on the mission.* I try to hold the images of bright, playful creatures in my mind as I wave my tail, speeding back up and heading for my destination. But dark thoughts keep creeping back in, staining the happiness burbling forth. *Many of those cute little critters will eventually die off if the oceans continue warming. There might be nothing where you're headed. It might be too late, and you'll have spent years on this effort only to confirm what you already fear the most: we've killed off the last of the white sharks.*

A roiling, selfish cloud of frustration settles over me. I just want to enjoy ten minutes of unvarnished freedom. Haven't I earned it, working hard these past few years? Every moment we haven't spent on Bruce has been spent in talks given to universities, to diving clubs, to elementary schools. Filmed, captioned, and shared online to improve accessibility and reach a wider audience whenever we could get permission.

We spoke with anyone who would have us, though we kept Bruce secret. We'd have loved to share each step in his development along the way, but our investors—the company whose animal interface technology we're testing as part of our funding agreement—insisted we keep the project hidden during development.

If this trip is successful, Deng will edit the footage. Once our investors give the go-ahead, we'll share what we have with the world. We'll compile everything, slapping on bite-sized slogans to hook viewers so that we can get to the real, sincere, earnest talks. The interviews we've been recording with oceanographers and deep-sea divers. Lab tests done by a salinity expert. Footage of the whales who beached themselves thanks to the volume of underwater missile testing, so excruciating to their sensitive ears that they'd rather suffer a painful death on land than stay underwater for a moment longer.

None of us is a fan of the sensationalism of many documentaries out there, using worst-case scenarios and spun figures taken out of context to spur people into action for a few moments that don't linger. There's enough real danger that we don't need to exaggerate. We want to drive continuous, sustained action. Ours will be not a single documentary, but an ongoing, interactive series. Maybe it'll be just as ineffective as the rest, but we're hoping Bruce will be enough of a splash to get people interested.

Nearing your destination, Callista says in my head.

I swim the last stretch, silently hoping we didn't do this all for nothing.

The White Shark Café is halfway between California and Hawaii, a spot unofficially named by Stanford researchers decades back. The satellite tags they used to track four white sharks found them travelling frequently to a spot centered at 23.37°N 132.71°W. It once housed a diverse food chain, rich in nutrients—and mating partners—for white sharks, but none have been seen here for years. From time to time, we've heard rumblings about sending a submersible down to the Café, but it never seems to happen. There are too many ecological crises and too many endangered species, but never enough funding to go around.

What if we do find a white shark, and it tries to mate with you? Deng joked when we settled on the spot. I tried not to think about the taste of the word *mate* in his mouth as I sent back a quip. Something along the lines of *let's hope none of them have necrophiliac tendencies.*

As I approach, proverbial breath held, it's clear that won't be a problem. There are no white sharks in sight.

Nothing yet, I tell Callista, mostly to break the mental silence. She and Deng must be as tense as I am.

Look around, she says.

Aye aye, cap. There are other types of sharks here. A shortfin mako speeds past, zipping out of sight before I can inspect it further. It's exciting to glimpse it here—even if shortfin makos don't top the endangered list. I swerve to avoid a large jellyfish undulating by. Fish of numerous species and sizes mix in the Café.

After spending some time circling the area, I catch sight of a blue shark descending into the depths, probably in search of food. It's about half my length, and bears signs of mating scars in the form of bite wounds; a mature female, then. I hear a sob from Callista, and know if I were in my human body, I would be welling up with tears right now. *We haven't killed them all.* Blue sharks, once an abundant species on the planet, are now critically endangered and thought by some to be extinct. They were heavily fished for their fins, their bodies often thrown back into the ocean to rot.

Our trip has already been worthwhile. I relax slightly.

Callista's maternal grandfather was a restaurant owner who served shark fin soup every weekend at wedding banquets. Before trawling was banned worldwide, Callista's father worked in the seafood industry, tossing unwanted animals back into the ocean after they'd been caught in massive nets. They may not be her sins, but more than the rest of us, she feels the weight of everything her ancestors contributed to the ocean's decline. As a kid, she tried every tactic she could think of to convince her grandparents to stop serving shark fin soup. In doing so, she fell in love with the creature she desperately wanted them to care about: the blue shark.

Tag it? I ask, and Callista hesitates. We've equipped Bruce to fire tags if needed, so we can track migration patterns. But we're here to reintroduce sharks to the world. How would it look if the first thing we do is show us shooting tag darts at them, even if it's for research?

No, she says, and it's probably too late anyway. The blue shark is out of sight. *At least we got footage.*

Yeah, I agree. *Good footage, hopefully. How much time left?*

Just under an hour before you need to head back. Your heat regulation is running through its power pretty fast down there. But you can come back at any time. We can always try again tomorrow.

I continue swimming.

It's only when I've finally given up and resigned myself to the return trip that I spot her.

She swims below me, a deep blue hue that barely stands out from the color of the ocean. This far down, where most colors of the spectrum aren't visible, everything is tinged various shades of blue. I feel a chill, impossible as I know it is in Bruce's skin.

See her? I think-whisper to Callista, as if our conversation might spook the shark.

Yeah! Holy shit, she's a beaut.

I follow, heart pounding.

Don't go too fast! Callista reminds me. *And don't stay too long. You're low on fuel.*

I know. But as I follow the white shark down to a thousand feet below the surface, I don't know if I'll ever be able to tear myself away. I've seen videos of white sharks, of course. And I've been swimming as Bruce for a year. But watching her up close makes everything about my movements look clunky, like an animatronic, or one of those ancient stop motion movies.

I can see her muscles ripple as she cuts through the water. There's a playfulness to her movements that belies the terrifying sight of her massively muscular body; or perhaps I'm too stuck viewing her through a human lens to understand the inherent alienness of the creature before me.

Though of course, in this domain where she reigns supreme, we are the aliens.

She speeds up, vanishing from sight, and I'm left looking desperately for her. We already have the footage, but...what if she's not here when we return tomorrow? What if she moves on to another region? What if I never see her again?

And then suddenly she's before me, so close we're nearly nose to nose. The first white shark anyone has seen in years. In my human body, I'd be drawing in a huge, nervous breath right now. As a shark, I merely stare and hope.

Holy shit! Callista says.

Holy shit, I agree.

Oh my god. Look at her underside, Callista says.

I do, staring at her belly, which would be white higher up in the water but this far down is merely lighter blue. I stare at the proportions, all wrong, her light underside bigger than those of the models. My first instinct is to be afraid. What if she consumed trash humans threw into the ocean and got an infection? She looks healthy, and . . . .

Oh my god.

She's pregnant! I shout the word in my head, startling myself with a jubilance so strong it's like it's my own pregnancy I'm announcing. A seed of hope, tender and fragile, blooms in my heart like a little green stalk poking up through hardened dirt. There's hope yet.

Despite us, the white sharks might survive.

She turns tail and swims off and I follow her, eager as a lover. Without speaking her language, I don't know if she wants me along for the ride or if she's indifferent, but she doesn't try to get rid of me. Trailing behind her, I listen to Callista's uncharacteristic chatter in my head. *We did it! We're following you in the boat, Ally. Oh my god, I can't believe we did it! I wonder how many pups she's carrying. Five? More?*

We cover the terrain together, leaving the Café far behind. We swim so quickly that everything feels like a blur and it's all I can do to keep my focus on her, not to lose her. Just me and the unnamed female shark. The ocean is ours.

Ahead of us, the water begins to vibrate.

The net comes of out nowhere, scooping her up. I barely miss getting caught in it myself, and the edge of the rope skims my skin. I scream as I see her fight to break free, dashing ahead. I can hear Callista cursing, her horrified shouts mixing with my own panic as I swim after the net.

Those fuckers! Deng is calling the coast guard!

It'll be too late, I think, following the net desperately. I watch, helpless, as the shark thrashes against the ropes that press into her side, packing her indiscriminately in with countless confused fish and bits of sharp, torn coral from the ocean floor. As the bottom-trawling net drags by, it leaves behind a trail of flattened land, destroying the natural landmarks many marine animals use to navigate the ocean.

I open my jaws and aim for a spot in the net near her, thrusting forward with all the power in my synthmuscles before clamping down on the netting.

Blood fills the water as my bite catches some of the fish in the net, severing their heads. Powerful as my massive jaws are, they're nothing against the motorized forward momentum of the illegal fishing vessel. It drags me along, teeth still locked around the net. I shake my head vigorously back and forth, trying to saw at the rope, but it's built to withstand worse, and my teeth were made for sinking into the soft flesh of fish and seals, not the tight twine of thick rope. Meanwhile, Callista's updates run through my head.

We're too far off the coast. They can't get here for hours.

I let go and try again. The water is heavy with fish blood, and the shark begins to thrash harder, snapping her jaws wildly. The scent of fish guts is likely overwhelming her, telling her it's time to feed. I manage to tear the rope in a few spots, and a few smaller fish stream out through the opening. I saw and bite again, and somehow manage to open a few more spots, even as my attacks continue to fill the water with the dizzying scent of death.

We'll be at your coordinates in about fifteen minutes. Deng has his equipment ready to film the trawling ship. Are you okay?

Fine. Stay out of sight. And be careful!

We all know that if the trawlers find us here, witnesses to their crimes, they're likely to shoot us. And if they discover a white shark in their net? She'll be their prize, sold captive to a collector for a king's ransom or, if they find her dead, stuffed and added to someone's private display.

If I were in my human body, tears of frustration would be filling my eyes. Instead, all I can do is try again. At the thought, I realize I've been a fool. I'm acting on instinct, keeping the shark in my sight. But trawling nets are a human problem, and I need to think like a human. Quickly, I swim up to the line attached to the ship. Disconnect the net first, *then* get her out.

I try and try but this line is much thicker than the netting, and my shark's teeth, so terrifying to humans, are nothing against the dense rope. It's like trying to saw through a tree with a shard of broken glass.

Fuck fuckfuck*fuck!*

When I return to the net, the shark is stuck fast. Her fins are tangled up in the rope, lines on her skin rubbed raw. She's cut up where the broken coral has pressed into her. I've barely made a dent in the rope. There's no fucking way I'm going to get her out this way.

I watch, feeling more helpless than ever, as human greed swallows up the only evidence we've had in years that wild white sharks still exist. She's pregnant, almost fully gestated, no small feat for a species that spends a year in the womb. She's proof that there are more sharks out there—at the very least, the shark who impregnated her—and she feels like the last chance we have of knowing there will be more of them to come.

I can't give up now.

Ally? What's going on?

Deng's last words to me fill my mind, echoed by the promise I made him. I wrench my thoughts away, heart already hurting at the choice ahead.

We assume human life is more valuable than any other kind. But is that still true when there's eight billion of us and only a smattering of them?

Ally? Hello?

Does the math still hold when there's an abundance of humans and a scarcity of sharks?

Ally? What's going on?

I don't want to do it. My thirty-five years don't feel like enough.

There's a crackle, and then the soft baritone of Deng's voice. *Ally Elizabeth Chen.* My heart skips a beat. I can hear the panic, barely masked beneath each syllable of my name. *Don't do this. Please.* He knows me too well, because he'd do the same in my position, and I in his. He knows.

I'm sorry, I whisper. Unspoken words ache in my throat. I know if I let him keep talking, he'll talk me out of it.

Before I can change my mind, I activate the function we all hoped I'd never have to use, doing my best to tune out Deng's pleas as I'm untethered from the simulacrum. A jolt of adrenaline shoots into my system as Bruce opens up and jettisons my body—my human body—into the cold, unforgiving water.

The air tank goes with me, part of the precautions we take. It takes all of my willpower to breathe steadily; gulping air could form an air bubble that paralyzes or kills me. I have just enough oxygen left to get to the surface safely, spending the proper amount of time at each depth interval. At the top, I can inflate my vest and wait for Deng and Callista to arrive. They'll be at my coordinates in ten minutes. All I have to do is go up.

I swim down, chasing the dragging net and the shark tangled inside. With each movement of my muscles, I feel the shock of going from interface gel to cold water. Silently, I beg any being out there listening to *please don't let me cramp up, not now*. Reaching into the pack strapped to my back, I pull out a diver's knife and begin to saw.

My fingers feel tight and raw as I grip the rope, whittling away at each strand, cutting through piece by piece. The knife slips, slicing through my skinsuit and cutting into my arm. Pain floods me, and I barely hold back a scream; afraid my mouthpiece will fall out. Gritting my teeth over the mouthpiece, I continue to saw strategically until at last, the rope begins to come apart.

Carefully, I make my way over to the shark, who stares at me through alien eyes. She blinks from the bottom up, a movement that feels disorienting. I force myself to look at her wounds as a primal fear urges me to leave, *now*. A part of me finally understands why all humans fear her kind.

I watch her as I cut through the ropes, carefully cutting away the piece binding her fins and lower body first. Eventually, I make my way to her jaws.

It's a mistake to check my air gauge when I already know what it'll say, but part of me can't help it. Even if Deng started putting his gear on as soon as we talked, even if Callista has sped her way to me the entire time, even if Deng jumps in the water as soon as they're in range, it'll be too late.

Two minutes.

It occurs to me that my arm is bleeding. There's blood in the water, and I'm weakened prey, ripe for the taking.

My last sight might be the inside of a shark's mouth.

I saw away the last of the entangled rope, using my remaining strength to pull it free from her, as gently as possible. She bursts through the hole in the net, wounded from coral cuts and rope burns. I hope that someday they'll scar, because it will mean she's survived this. That she's survived us.

As the last of my air runs out, I watch her muscular tail bend back and forth, propelling her with incredible speed.

She swims away, into the dark waters, injured but free.

Kelsea Yu is a Taiwanese Chinese American writer and mother living in the Pacific Northwest. She's eternally enthusiastic about sharks and appreciates a good ghost story. Her debut novella, *Bound Feet*, is published by Cemetery Gates Media, and her upcoming novella, *The Bones Beneath Paris*, will be published by Dark Matter Ink. Her debut novel will be released by Bloomsbury Children's in 2024. Kelsea's short stories are forthcoming or published in *Fantasy*, *PseudoPod*, and *Kaleidotrope*, and in various anthologies. Find Kelsea on Instagram or Twitter as @anovelescape or visit her website kelseayu.com.

SQUAWKER AND DOLPHIN SWIMMING TOGETHER

T. K. Rex

The Submersible aQuatic Cetacean Communication Robot—professionally known as SQCCR, affectionately known as "Squawker"—splashes into the harbor from the starboard side of the *Charlotte's Web* at dawn. A few brilliant, cool drops hit Julia's skin.

The heat index is already 96 and aiming for the red by ten. What must the dolphins think of the extra three degrees the world's gained since the oldest members of their pods were born?

Maybe this is the upgrade that will finally help her find out.

"Everything's looking good," Parviz says through the radio, from his station by the monitors back at the lab. "Hey I'm hearing some signature whistles—it's the ladies. They're not too far from you."

Julia scans the gentle blue-green waves for them, from the causeway in the distance to the houseboats down in Punta Gorda, where there were houses just ten years ago.

"There they are!" Tumelo says, pointing west with their chin. Julia's grad student from Botswana is taller than her, even more than most people are, with a frohawk, a kind heart and a gift for 3D modeling.

Julia can see the pod, dorsal fins cutting through the shining surface of the bay, spouts and splashes getting closer. Parviz comes in on radio, "Whoa, they're already approaching. That was fast."

Time to get back to the lab. She misses the days of working directly with the dolphins, but it's better for them this way.

As the *Charlotte's Web* turns around and picks up speed, she catches a glimpse of them below the surface. Ten female Atlantic bottlenose dolphins, gray and sleek and strong, with their three calves. The mammals swim against, around each other, close and then apart and close again, one leaps, another leaps, three more surface to exhale.

Tumelo grins wide at Julia, then looks back out at the water, where just below the surface a dolphin is already swimming right up to the drone. "That must be Summer," Tumelo says.

Julia nods. Summer's the only one who hasn't lost interest in Squawker.

Parviz confirms. "She's definitely saying something—" a few clicks and whistles filter through his pause. "It's processing...." It's not physically possible to be any sweatier, but Julia's palms somehow feel even slicker than they did a minute ago. Is this it? "Oh shit," Parviz says. "The new visuals are *way* better."

Julia's heart pounds in her chest like a storm. Tumelo grabs her arm, grip strong and smile wide.

"What are you seeing?!" Julia asks.

"Uhh... It looks like Squawker! It looks a *lot* like Squawker. She's literally sending us a portrait. It's crystal clear, Jules. Damn. We nailed it this time." Victory and wonder in his voice.

"Yes! We finally did it!" Tumelo jumps up and down with excitement. "Oh, I would hug you if it wasn't so hot!"

Julia laughs and cheers with her team. Two decades of work have led to this. The hardware, the algorithms, the past three years of fine-tuning... all so she could see the dolphins' sounds the way the dolphins do, in three dimensions. She can't wait to get back to the lab and look at the results herself.

After a lifetime of wondering, she's finally going to know exactly what they're saying.

What will she say back?

That night, instead of going home, they look at all the footage and the readouts from the afternoon another dozen times. Tumelo picks up samosas and biryani from the place across the street and Anusha brings Prosecco. Parviz runs '30s pop songs through the visualizer until Anusha drives him home. By 2am Tumelo and Julia are still there, looking over everything, just one more time.

"Right here," Tumelo says, pointing at a monitor. "That's the drone."

"I wonder," Julia says, leaning on the back of Tumelo's chair, "if we have enough data with this yet to compose an original message. Not just mimicry."

"Oh." They nod enthusiastically. "I think we do. We've got the drone, and the dolphin, and the boat, and I still think those things are fish.... And then there's all this stuff that we just have no idea what it is." They grin, gesturing to the incomprehensible forms swirling on the third monitor.

"What do you think of it? Honestly."

"I think... it's beautiful. It could be pure expression, play, something we're not calibrated for...."

"Abstraction?"

Tumelo laughs. "Anusha definitely thinks so."

"But do *you* think so? *Tursiops* has been around at least five million years, and the dolphin braincase has barely changed in twelve million. They've had the biology to communicate with this level of complexity six times longer than we've been capable of spoken language. We *know* they have the mental capacity. We *know* they're capable of abstract thought. And now we finally have a way of teasing out which words are literal representations of our world, and which aren't. *Those* are the ones I want to understand next, Tumelo."

"I'm with you, Dr. Redhearth. It's all very exciting."

Julia swallows the last of her warm prosecco. "You're bilingual."

"Trilingual, actually," Tumelo grins. "Why?"

"Nice. So you know how learning a new language expands the way you see the world, the concepts you have access to."

"Oh definitely."

"Imagine what new concepts they could bring into our world, Tumelo."

"Or us to theirs, Dr. Redhearth."

True. Julia nods and thinks of all the trash in Charlotte Harbor. All the violence in the news. The extremists and the propaganda, the dead zones in the Gulf.... But maybe... maybe an outside perspective is just the thing the human world needs.

Or another glass of Prosecco. She pours the last splash of the last bottle out into each of their mugs. "To Summer."

"To Summer." Tumelo smiles warmly.

It's room temperature and flat. What had they been talking about before the dread seeped in? Something about how long dolphins have been capable of language. "You know," Julia says, swirling her mug, "they've had time to evolve their languages into things we might not even understand. Nam-shubs, obscure allegories, ways of communicating we've only imagined in science fiction."

"Look at you, Dr. Redhearth, getting into the telepathic dolphin comment thread! If the Redditors could see you now!"

Julia laughs heartily. "I am *not* saying they're telepathic! But since you went there, we know they can target sound like a laser beam, right? So what's stopping them from triggering the speech centers of the brain directly and making us hear English words, with enough practice? I'm just saying!"

"You're just tipsy, is what you are!"

"That. Is true."

"Listen, Julia. Tomorrow, I'm going to start composing our first original animation. And we're going to finally prove to Summer that our little Squawker isn't just a novelty. And then, one piece at a time, we'll figure out what all that other . . . *stuff* . . . is. Tonight, you better call a car, OK?"

"Tomorrow's Saturday."

"And?"

The whole team is at the research center, glued to the monitors streaming Squawker's feed. Summer's smooth, gray form fills the video, and her usual chatter streams in through the speakers. It'll take time to process that part of the conversation, but right now, Julia is trying to remember to breathe, palms sweating, waiting for a momentary lull in Summer's monologue to press the button. To share, for the first time, something in Summer's language that isn't merely mimicry.

And then it's there, the break, and Summer waits. Usually this is when they play what she just said back to her, and they go back and forth till she gets bored or the other dolphins call her away. But this time, Julia hits the key that plays the statement they spent a solid week composing out of scraps of sound, testing and retesting to make sure it reproduced in three dimensions as intended.

On the screen, it looks like what she hopes Summer sees: a 3D rendering of Squawker and a dolphin in motion, swimming together. The computer generates the caption: SQUAWKER AND DOLPHIN SWIMMING TOGETHER. The sound is just a set of squeaks, indistinguishable to Julia's ears from thousands she's heard before, most of it outside her hearing range entirely.

What follows is a moment of curious silence, Summer turning her head to look at Squawker closely with one eye, then swimming around it, examining it the way she did the first time she met the drone two years ago. The gathered scientists all hold their breath.

Then a barrage of squeaks and whistles, and Julia thinks she recognizes the same squeak they just sent, repeated several times, but she can't be sure.

The translation comes in. A perfect 3D rendering of Squawker and a dolphin swimming side by side. The machine translation captions: SQUAWKER AND DOLPHIN SWIMMING TOGETHER.

There's so much to analyze here, Julia's thinking, as a murmur rises, and becomes a cheer, and Parviz starts high-fiving everybody. Tumelo, grinning wide, asks Julia if they should draft a press release.

Before Julia can even wrap her head around that, Summer swims away abruptly.

"Oh shit, we didn't scare her off, did we?" Parviz asks.

"Not this dolphin, she's fearless," says Tumelo.

"She's telling the pod. Look," Anusha says, and points to the Camera 5 monitor with a slender hand and an eager sparkle in her black-lined eyes. In the distance, Summer joins the pod, and the speakers all around the room play their faint, far away chatter.

Julia is certain she hears sounds that make up SQUAWKER AND DOLPHIN SWIMMING TOGETHER repeated among the pod. Summer's telling them what the drone said, she has to be.

It's working. Real communication is finally possible. The weight of so many years of doubt starts lifting.

But what happens now? For a moment she feels almost dizzy.

The pod follows Summer back to Squawker. Summer whistles at the drone, and Julia would give anything to know what she's saying right now, but there's a short delay in processing. For now, there's only one response. Julia hits send.

SQUAWKER AND DOLPHIN SWIMMING TOGETHER.

The pod erupts in chatter. So many speaking so fast simultaneously they'll never pick it all apart.

Later, analyzing everything, Summer's parting phrase that day stands out. It's a vivid image of herself and Squawker swimming side by side, just like in the message they sent, but now surrounded by the pod. In the recording, Squawker has no reply. But Summer waits. She waits until the pod begins to leave, and call for her, and then she finally, slowly, turns and swims away.

POD SWIMMING. FISH. POD CHASING FISH. CATCHING FISH. EATING FISH. SQUAWKER EATING FISH.

Julia only has so many phrases to respond with. She pulls up the new VR interface Parviz designed and adds a file from the weather category they explored last week.

SQUAWKER EATING SUN. She makes up for the drone's lack of a mouth by simply having it absorb the sun, swallowing it whole through its solar panel fins.

Summer gives the drone a sort of side-eye. SUN, she repeats. Incredulous, maybe? Then a string the computer isn't confident about but might be a dolphin jumping so high it gets lost in the clouds. Julia laughs. That can't be it, but wow. It's almost a joke, almost a fable. Could they really have those? Anything is starting to seem possible.

In a stroke of insight, she commands the drone to surface and start charging up its solar fins. Through its cameras, Julia floats virtually upward through the green, wet world that surrounds her in VR. Summer follows, chattering so many things so fast the computer can't keep up. When the fins unfurl, Summer squeaks, and the computer catches: SQUAWKER EATING SUN. SQUAWKER EATING SUN. SQUAWKER EATING SUN.

Julia wants to try something else. SQUAWKER, HUMAN. The human form she picks is a bit of public domain 3D clip art, a blonde woman in a bikini, frozen in a front crawl stroke.

Summer's response makes her laugh out loud. SQUAWKER EATING HUMAN.

SQUAWKER AND HUMAN SWIMMING TOGETHER, she replies.

HUMAN, BOAT, [UNINTELLIGIBLE]. NETS. FISH GOING UP. [UNINTELLIGIBLE] DOLPHINS AND HUMANS SWIMMING TOGETHER. [UNINTELLIGIBLE] HUMAN SHOOTING AT DOLPHINS FROM BOAT.

The last image isn't one she's seen before from Summer, but it's clear as day, the gun is there in the man's hands and the shockwave of the gunshots distorts the whole thing in a sudden burst. The machine translation is dead on.

A few years ago some drunk asshole took his motorboat out into the harbor and started shooting at the dolphins playing in his wake. Two females were injured, and a calf was killed. Julia was livid. The whole mess sped up the team's decision to use drones exclusively, to keep the dolphins from getting too comfortable around boats, from forming any relationship with humans at all.

Summer's expression of the event chills Julia. Not just because they both remember the same painful incident, and not just because it's finally proof dolphins can translate what they see above the water into 3D burst-pulse language. The thing that feels like a storm surge on a doorstep is the fact it wasn't even Summer's pod.

And Summer isn't done. DOLPHINS SINKING. [UNINTELLIGIBLE]. She claps her jaw, flashing pointed teeth.

That's a threat behavior. Julia replies with: DOLPHIN SWIMMING. HUMAN SWIMMING. SQUAWKER SWIMMING. HUMAN DOLPHIN AND SQUAWKER SWIMMING TOGETHER.

Summer replies, adding her own signature whistle to the established dolphin form: SUMMER-DOLPHIN AND SQUAWKER SWIMMING TOGETHER. She doesn't mention humans.

"I guess I don't blame you, Summer," she mutters to the monitors. "We've been dicks, haven't we?" The shooter in the motorboat didn't even go to jail. He didn't even lose his boat. He didn't even lose his gun. She wants to believe that would have gone differently if it had been a human child killed, but this is Florida, after all.

She tries to keep the abstract as downplayed as possible, but everyone sees through it. The moment it's up on the conference website, Julia starts getting messages from colleagues.

"You did it, didn't you?"

"Is this what I think it is?"

"Holy shit I can't wait to see this talk."

"I'm literally imagining you showing up on that stage with a dolphin in some kind of land suit, please tell me that's your plan, Julia!"

Even the most well-meaning responses from people she's known for years make her palms sweat when she sees them.

She's jet lagged from the flight to Vancouver, and nervous on the stage the way she always is, but when Summer's picture comes up on the screen she can't help but smile.

"And that's Summer, interacting with our drone this past July, a few weeks after the upgrades. And now I'll play some clips from our conversation that day."

She goes to the next slide, and the squeaks and buzzes of burst-pulses fill the hall from every speaker, while the 3D animation of their meaning plays, overlaid on the video of Summer holding a fish between her teeth. FISH, the caption says, with Summer's perfect 3D render of the creature she just caught. FISH, the drone repeats. They do the same with SNAIL, BEER CAN, and SCALLOP.

After apparently finishing the lesson to Summer's satisfaction, Squawker says, CHRYSANTHEMUM. Tumelo made the 3D render from a scan they'd taken at a diner table when the team was out for lunch.

"We wanted to see what she would do with something she's

never observed before."

Summer swims away.

"Wait for it . . . ."

She comes back a moment later with a sea urchin clinging to a frayed yard of orange rope. It does resemble the chrysanthemum, as much as anything in Charlotte Harbor. The crowd laughs, then starts applauding.

By the time her talk is over and the line for questions stretches out the door, she feels a thick accomplishment set in like cooling rain. Her cheeks begin to ache from smiling.

She calls on the first person in line, one of the young cynics who gave a talk last year on how it's probably all pretty nonsense, just like birdsong.

"All the so-called 'words' you've shown us today are still basically mimicry," he says. "No different from a lyre bird replicating the sound of a chainsaw. So, I applaud you for finally getting these images into focus, but is there any indication in any of this that the dolphins are doing anything but playing?"

And what's so wrong with that? Deep breath, Julia. Be nice. "There is," she answers calmly. "Most of what we're picking up from the rest of the pod is still unintelligible. Can we definitively say everything we don't understand is something profound? Of course not. A lot of it is probably gossip, which we know humans use for social bonding. Some of it is probably fun nonsense, the way we make up words when we sing. The big breakthrough here is that now, with a few words we *do* understand, we can start to learn the rest. Next question."

An older man she's only met a couple times is next. "Well, this is more of a comment than a question." A few groans come from the audience. "This research is very interesting, and if it can be successfully replicated with more than one dolphin, I have to say it seems like it might be enough to start seeking legal personhood again." A few people clap, most nod.

"You might be right. I hope you're right." Julia shrugs and smiles. "Who knows, maybe this time next year it'll be Summer up here doing the presenting."

Polite laughter. Everyone here knows it'll be years before they understand the language enough for Summer or some other dolphin to declare their personhood, without ambiguity, in a court of law.

And even then, laws tend to wait as long as possible to change.

The whole team gathers after, greeting her with high fives and hugs outside the conference center. "Drinks on me!" Parviz declares, and belts out a sea shanty as they walk along Vancouver Harbor to the hotel bar.

Oh what do you do with a talking dolphin?
What do you do with a talking dolphin?
What do you do with a talking dolphin?
Register her to voooote

Anusha, still laughing at Parviz's antics, stops and leans over the rail, pointing out at the water. "Look, orcas!"

They all stop and look. Julia sees a spout, then three tall black dorsal fins, out near the bare wood spires of a sunken forest. It was still an island last time she was here.

Tumelo declares heartily, "They send their congratulations, Dr. Redhearth!"

"I wonder if we could explain all this somehow to Summer when we get back?" Anusha muses, tracing a slow line across the condensation of her beer glass. The water drips on to the reclaimed wood of their corner table.

Behind Anusha, up above the bar, someone's set the television to a news station, which Julia has more or less successfully ignored all night.

"Yes! I could throw together a whole sequence for her," Tumelo says. "I wonder how much of it would make sense to her though?"

"I bet she thinks airplanes are some kind of bird," Parviz says.

Anusha laughs a little. "I think she knows they're machines. When they fly low? All that noise? Come on."

"But does she know what a machine is? Does she know Squawker is a machine?" Parviz counters, and finishes his third glass.

The television centers in on Florida. A red trajectory cone that was pointed at the panhandle yesterday has shifted south. Way south.

"Shit."

The others follow her gaze.

The meteorologist's voice finds its way across the bar to them, "This might remind some of our long-time viewers of Ian back in '22, or even Charley in '04, if you were around back then—"

"Checking our flight." Parviz already has his phone out. A moment later they all get the notification: canceled.

"What do we do?" Tumelo asks. "I'm from a landlocked country."

"Do we have someone who can go to the lab and get the hurricane shutters down?" Anusha asks.

Julia nods, already swiping through her contacts.

The room she's splitting with Anusha has two oversized blue beds, stylized wall art of orcas and salmon by a local indigenous printmaker, and an inset television that takes up most of the widest wall.

All they can do is watch.

Watch as the too-warm water of the Gulf of Mexico feeds the hurricane enough to grow from category four to category five.

And in the morning, after barely sleeping, all they can do is watch, still in their pajamas, Anusha's hand over her mouth in shock, Julia too frozen with her arm around Anusha to answer Tumelo's knock on their door, as a category six makes landfall.

Julia's mom has a hundred million mugs. There's one from their Grand Canyon trip when she was nine, one each from all five tech companies Mom built apps for in the '20s, and of course the one from Bermuda that Julia gave her when she went for research as a grad student. There's a dolphin on it. Like her favorite Florida mug back at the lab. The one that's probably at the bottom of Charlotte

Harbor now with everything else.

Julia pushes the dolphin mug back into the crowd and grabs the two handmade ones they found at a garage sale once when she was seventeen. She fills them up with coffee and meets Mom out on the side deck, where the late-spring sun has warmed the air enough that she can barely see the steam rise off their drinks.

"Ooh, you brought coffee! See, this is why you're my favorite."

"Ha. I'm your only." She can't quite bring herself to smile back, but she tries.

"You know I think I saw a fluke out there," Mom says, pointing with her chin while she cups the hot mug with both hands. "Couple spouts."

To the west, past a swathe of blooming coastal prairie and a grove of twisty windblown pines, the cold Pacific Ocean crashes into the state of Oregon, gnawing off a chunk with every wave.

Julia grunts, and sips her coffee, leaning back into the wooden deck chair.

"You know," Mom says, "They still do those whale watching trips I used to take you on in town. Different folks running it, nice couple though. I could book us—"

"Mom, stop. I don't want to go whale watching."

"I know." Mom sighs. "You're depressed. I get it." She sets her mug down on the little rusting table that she's kept out here for twenty years. "But honey, this is your life's work. You've got to get back up on your feet. It's been six months."

"Are you sick of me already?"

"Never! But Julia, seriously. There has to be something you can do instead of sitting around here playing video games all day."

"I'm not. . . ." Who is she kidding? Every few days she brings out a VR headset with the intention of re-watching Squawker's old recordings, the ones saved to the cloud, taking notes or something, maybe getting a new insight. But every time she puts it on, she stares at the folder for a few minutes, and inevitably opens *Elder Scrolls VII* instead, where she can be a hot elf mage with easily definable and imminently achievable problems to solve for the rest of the day.

"Yeah I thought so," Mom replies to Julia's trailed-off thought.

DOLPHIN SINKING.

"What's the point, Mom? What's the fucking point of trying to talk to dolphins when people are killed and displaced by the millions in these floods, and storms, and fires, and plagues? Every fucking year. I should be helping with the rewilding efforts out here, or doing climate science, or joining the protests or doing eco-terrorism, *anything*, anything that actually might help slow this planet's fucking freefall."

"Honey," Mom says. "Leave the 'eco-terrorism' to the pros." She winks. Julia suddenly wonders where she really was all last week, but before she can finish that thought, Mom continues, "I can't believe I'm the one who has to tell *you* this, but dolphins are people too. And we share the same fucked up world. And *they still need you.*"

How can I help anybody when I'm the one drowning?

Julia's phone vibrates in the pocket of her sweatpants. She sighs and takes a peek. Parviz. He's been volunteering with the recovery effort since it started, texting her photos every few days that she can't bear to look at. But this time it's a phone call.

"Answer it!" Mom says.

She rolls her eyes, and does.

"Jules!" Parviz sounds different. Brighter. Sober. "You're not gonna believe it. We found Squawker!"

The *Charlotte's Web*, patched up from its encounter with a downtown Punta Gorda sports bar, sputters to a slow drift out near the debris-strewn strip of sand that was Boca Grande a year ago.

Parviz leans on the rail by Julia, joining her in awe of the destruction. There are no words for it.

But it's not why they're here.

"Wish Tumelo was with us for this," he says.

"I'm working on their visa," Julia replies, brushing a windblown curl out of her eyes. "If this is our pod, maybe we can get some funding, speed it up a little."

Assuming the pod made it through the storm. Assuming Summer, or any of them, still remembers Squawker. Assuming any dolphin gives a shit and has the patience to start teaching them again.

"Hey!" Anusha yells from the cabin, pulling her headphones to the side. "I got the signature whistles! Three matches so far!"

If one of them was Summer, Anusha would have said so. Julia's heart starts pounding anyway. Any familiar dolphin is better than none, and they were all interested in Squawker at first. Maybe it's been long enough the novelty effect will work again.

But Summer.... She might still turn up. No reason to assume the worst.

"There they are!" Parviz points and grins wide.

Julia sees them. Three dorsal fins slip through the water, then another two, one so small it's barely visible. A new calf.

She wonders what the little one's signature whistle sounds like.

"They're gonna be so stoked to see Squawker again," Parviz says.

Where's Summer?

When the drone is in the water, Julia heads to the cabin, where Anusha hands her the headset and makes room on the small bench. Their new onboard equipment is a joke compared to what they lost, but it's all they can afford for now, and the *Charlotte's Web* is the closest thing they have left to a lab.

Through Squawker's cameras, she sees the dolphins in the distance. And the rubble on the sea floor, stretching as far as the blue-gray visibility allows today. Mailboxes, planks of wood, entire cars, palm trees with dead algae-laden fronds still on them, swaying in the current where they stick out from the sand.

And a few fish. Maybe, if the Gulf wasn't too warm and too acidic, a coral reef would grow out of the ruins, over time.

She sends out a call to the pod, an image of Squawker. Maybe someone will recognize it.

A couple dolphins turn to look, and she's hit with a barrage of echolocation clicks. One swims toward her, fast.

The rendered visuals are low poly and the translation lags, but the message is unmistakable.

SUMMER-DOLPHIN AND SQUAWKER SWIMMING TOGETHER.

It's her. Julia catches her relief in her throat. "It's her! It's

Summer!" she says out loud, and sends Summer's message back as quickly as she can. Parviz and Anusha cheer.

"I'm texting Tumelo!" Anusha says.

Summer slides against the drone excitedly, knocking it off-kilter for a moment in a dolphin version of a bear hug. Then she hovers in the water, in front of Squawker's front cameras, and unloads.

SUMMER-DOLPHIN SWIMMING [UNINTELLIGIBLE]. SHARKS EATING SQUAWKER. SQUAWKER CAUGHT IN NET. BOAT EATING SQUAWKER. HUMAN SHOOTING SQUAWKER.

Was she . . . worried about the drone? She goes on.

SUMMER-DOLPHIN ALONE, SWIMMING IN EVERY DIRECTION [LOW CONFIDENCE]. [UNINTELLIGIBLE]. BOATS SINKING. [UNINTELLIGIBLE]. HUMANS SINKING. DEBRIS [LOW CONFIDENCE] SINKING. TREES SINKING.

There's a layer to the visuals that looks like something from the weather category. This is what the hurricane was like for her, it has to be.

Summer still isn't done. SUMMER-DOLPHIN [UNINTELLIGIBLE] SQUAWKER. SUMMER-DOLPHIN LIFTING SQUAWKER TO THE SURFACE. [UNINTELLIGIBLE]. SQUAWKER [UNINTELLIGIBLE]. SQUAWKER SINKING. SUMMER-DOLPHIN [UNINTELLIGIBLE]. SUMMER-DOLPHIN PUSHING SQUAWKER TO LAND. SUMMER-DOLPHIN SWIMMING ALONE. [UNINTELLIGIBLE]. SUMMER-DOLPHIN WITH POD [UNINTELLIGIBLE].

"Damn, Summer." Parviz says. He must be watching the cabin monitor. "Am I seeing this right? Did she go looking for Squawker after the storm and . . . ."

"She tried to help it by lifting it up to the surface," Anusha says, in awe. "It's what she would do with a sick calf, but . . . she also knows Squawker eats sunlight."

"And then when Squawker still wouldn't talk to her, she brought it to shore," Julia says.

"Maybe thinking humans could help it?" Anusha wonders. "Maybe she knows we made it after all."

"We found Squawker on the beach near the lab," Parviz says.

"Fuck. This explains why no one noticed it on the first pass. She hadn't rescued it yet."

It takes a moment to sink in.

"How do dolphins thank each other?" Julia breathes.

No one has an answer. Not yet. Not for years, if years are something they still have.

She has far more to thank Summer for than just saving Squawker.

Getting back out here, facing all their ruined equipment, all the ruined lives and homes. Joining Parviz and Anusha in the volunteer efforts while they were waiting for the boat's repairs. Seeing the restaurant owners and fishermen and the people from the laundromat, all the neighbors of the lab who she never gave a second thought before, all working together to rebuild, stopping in the rubble to contain their sudden tears. She only came back to be a part of that because Summer saved her drone.

Summer's endless patience, curiosity, collaboration . . . they've kept Julia afloat so many times.

And the simple fact that Summer's always seemed to want to learn, to bridge the gap between them, just as much Julia . . . .

She leans against the hard wall of the cabin and bites her lower lip to hold back the tide of feelings.

Summer waits for her response, head cocked, eyes searching the cameras.

T. K. Rex (she/they) is a science fiction and fantasy author of European/Ashkenazi descent, living in San Francisco on Ohlone Ramaytush land. She gets her environmentalism from her Californian mother and her fascination with dolphins from her Floridian father. Recently, she attended the Clarion Writers Workshop in San Diego, and joined Mastodon as @tkrex@sfba.social. (You can still find her elsewhere as @tharkibo.) Her other eco-fiction short stories can be found in *Asimov's Science Fiction*, *Imagine 2200: Climate Fiction for Future Ancestors*, *Strange Horizons*, and *New Edge Sword and Sorcery*.

Photographer credit: Malcolm J. Brenner.

www.ingramcontent.com/pod-product-compliance
Lightning Source LLC
Chambersburg PA
CBHW061546210726
48287CB00006B/2090

* 9 7 8 1 9 5 5 3 6 0 0 9 8 *